FOXBOOK

Medieval & Contemporary Fables from Armenia

First Edition

Translated, compiled & edited by
Sar Kamler

2023

DUDUKHOUSE
An imprint of Dudukhouse Inc.
www.dudukhouse.com

Copyright © 2023 by Sar Kamler

All rights reserved. No part of this publication may be reproduced, distributed, or transmitted in any form or by any means, including photocopying, recording, or other electronic or mechanical methods, without the prior written permission of the publisher, except in the case of brief quotations embodied in critical reviews and certain other noncommercial uses permitted by copyright law.

ISBN 978-1-7388352-3-2 (Paperback)
ISBN 978-1-7388352-4-9 (Hardcover)

Official Website
www.thefoxbook.com

Set in EB Garamond
Designed by Sar Kamler
Illustrations by Midjourney AI

*To my family, friends and mentors,
whose wisdom radiates through their actions, stories, and essence,
illuminating the path I tread.*

With nothing we arrive...

TABLE OF CONTENTS

A FEW WORDS	1
TRACING THE ROOTS: A BRIEF HISTORY OF ARMENIAN FABLES	5
1. A DROP OF HONEY	17
2. THE OX AND THE HORSE	18
3. THE BUFFALO	19
4. THE CHICKEN AND THE MASTER	20
5. THE CHEETAH	22
6. THE CHURCH AND THE MILL	23
7. THE WISE MAN AND THE TREES	24
8. THE ANT	25
9. THE PARTRIDGE AND THE HUNTER	26
10. THE DONKEY IN LION'S SKIN	28
11. THE DOCTOR FROG	29
12. GOD AND HIS CREATIONS	32
13. THE FALCON AND THE PARTRIDGE	34
14. DOVE'S MEEKNESS	35
15. WISE CROWS	36
16. THE HAWKS AND THE EAGLES	37
17. THE WOLF AND THE LAMB	38
18. SPIDER	40
19. THE WOLF AND THE DONKEY	41
20. A MAN AND GARLIC	42
21. THE CRIPPLED LION	43
22. THE OX	44
23. THE LIONESS AND THE FOX	46
24. ARAMAZD AND THE SNAKE	47
25. THE CAMEL, THE WOLF, AND THE FOX	48
26. THE LION, THE WOLF AND THE FOX	49

27. THE SUNFLOWER	50
28. THE WIDOW AND THE PRIEST	52
29. THE BEAR AND THE ANT	53
30. THE DYING CAMEL	54
31. THE HOOPOE	56
32. THE HEDGEHOG AND THE HAMSTER	57
33. THE TURNIP AND THE CARROT	58
34. THE OWL AND THE EAGLE	59
35. THE FALCON AND THE DOVE	61
36. THE EAGLE	62
37. THE MERLIN AND THE RINGDOVE	63
38. THE BUFFALO - SURVEYOR	64
39. THE FOOL AND THE DOCTOR	65
40. THE WOLF AND THE SHEEP	67
41. THE THIEF	70
42. THE BEAR AND THE FOX	71
43. THE LION AND THE FOX	72
44. THE CONFESSION	74
45. THE MONKEY AND THE FISHERMAN	75
46. THE PRAYER OF THE WIDOW	76
47. THE WOLVES AND THE SHEEP	77
48. THE WIDOW AND HER SON	78
49. THE HEIFERS AND THE BULLS	80
50. A TRADER'S PRAYER	81
51. THE DROWNING DONKEY	82
52. THE TRUSTING WOLF	83
53. THE MOLE	85
54. THE BED OF A DEBTOR	86
55. THE FOX AND THE BAIT	87
56. THE DEER AND THE DOGS	88
57. THE ENVIOUS	90
58. THE ROOSTERS	91

59. PLATO AND THE BABY ELEPHANT	92
60. THE GOAT AND THE WOLF	93
61. THE ROOSTER AND THE KING	94
62. THE YOUNG WOLF AND THE ALPHABET	96
63. THE PIG AND THE KING	97
64. THE MAGPIE AND THE PRIEST	98
65. THE ILL-TEMPERED CAMEL	99
66. THE STORKS AND THE SPARROWS	100
67. THE BEAVER	102
68. THE SUN	103
69. THE FOX AND THE CRAWFISH	104
70. THE BUTTERFLIES	105
71. THE ROOSTER AND LAZY PEOPLE	106
72. THE COWS	108
73. THE CRAYFISH AND ITS YOUNG	109
74. AN OBSTINATE HORSE	112
75. GENEROSITY	113
76. THE FISH AND THE KING	115
77. THE POOR MAN AND THE WOLF	116
78. THE JUJUBE TREE AND THE FOOL	117
79. THE DONKEY AT THE WEDDING	118
80. THE BLACKSMITH AND THE CARPENTER	119
81. THE BLACKSMITH AND THE COPPERSMITH	121
82. A FLEA AND A PRINCE	122
83. A MAN AND A WATERMELON	123
84. THE FISH OR THE CAT	124
85. THE BANDIT AND THE PRIEST	126
86. THE FOX AND THE PARTRIDGE	127
87. THE BABY CAMEL, THE FOAL AND THE PIGS	128
88. THE MULE	129
89. THE MOON	130
90. THE BRAVE WARRIOR	132

91. THE PHILOSOPHER AT THE FEAST	133
92. THE OLD WARRIOR	134
93. THE WILD BOAR AND THE FOX	135
94. THE CAT AND THE MICE	137
95. THE OLD DONKEY	138
96. THE RAM	139
97. THE TURTLE AND THE HORSE	140
98. THE SHEEP AND THE GOATS	141
99. THE PEACOCK AND THE PIGEON	143
100. THE CABBAGE	144
101. THE PEACOCK AND EAGLE	145
102. THE DEATH OF THE EAGLE	146
103. LEVIATHAN	148
104. THE DECEIVED LION	149
105. TANNER AND FURRIER	150
106. THE FOX AND THE CAMEL	151
107. ALMOND AND CHESTNUT	152
108. THE WIDOW AND THE PRINCE	154
109. THE MAGPIE	155
110. SWALLOW'S NEST	156
111. A BEGGAR'S PRAYER	157
112. THE AXES AND THE TREES	159
113. THE PRIEST AND THE BIRDS	160
114. CUCUMBER AND MELON	161
115. DONKEY THE GRANDFATHER	162
116. THE SNAIL AND THE HEDGEHOG	164
117. THE LITTLE SPARROW	167
118. THE CAMELS AND THE FOXES	168
119. THE HYENA AND THE LION	169
120. THE BADGER AND THE FOX	170
121. THE ENCHANTED LION	172
122. THE FOX AND THE HUNTERS	173

123. THE CONFIDENT IGNORAMUS	174
124. THE POTTER'S DOG	175
125. THE RABBITS AND THE FROGS	177
126. THE COMBATIVE BULL	178
127. THE OSTRICH AND THE SPARROW	179
128. GOLD AND WHEAT	180
129. THE FOX AND THE DOGS	182
130. THE MARTEN AND THE MOUSE	183
131. THE WOLF AND THE FOX	184
132. THE PANTHER	185
133. THE BIRD AND THE HORSE	186
134. THE LIZARDS AND THE MOLE	188
135. THE WOLF, THE GAZELLE, AND THE LION	189
136. THE NAIVE THIEVES	190
137. THE WILL ABOUT THE TREASURE	191
138. THE REED AND THE TREES	193
139. THE FOX AND THE NOTE-BEARING WOLF	194
140. THE LION AND THE MAN	195
141. A MAN AND THE WOLF	196
142. THE CORRUPTED JUDGE AND THE JUG OF BUTTER	197
143. A MAN, A NUT AND A WATERMELON	199
144. RICH IN-LAW AND THE MAIDEN	200
145. THE FOX AND THE GEESE	201
146. THE HAWK AND THE DOMESTIC CHICKEN	202
147. THE HONOR OF ROBES	204
148. PRAYER OF A GREEDY MAN	205
149. THE PARABLE OF PATIENCE	206
150. ALEXANDER AND THE INDIAN ARCHER	207
151. THE POMEGRANATE AND THE FIG	208
152. THE RASPBERRY AND THE GRAPEVINE	210
153. THE PEACH AND THE QUINCE	211
154. THE COTTON AND THE PLANE TREE	212

155. THE STORK AND THE SPARROWS	213
156. THE MONKEY AND THE MIRROR	215
157. THE VILLAGE OF ASTRAY	218
158. THE POOR MAN AND THE GOLDEN EGG-LAYING TURKEY	219
159. THE FOX AND THE CROW WITH CHEESE	220
160. THE JACKDAW IN STRANGER'S FEATHERS	222
161. THE PRINCE AND THE FISH	223
162. PARTRIDGE	224
163. THE SICK LION AND THE HEARTLESS AND EARLESS DONKEY	225
164. THE FOX AND THE WOLF	227
165. THE FOX AND THE EAGLE	228
166. THE BOY AND THE CHICKEN	229
167. THE ANT AND THE DOVE	230
168. THE ANTS AND THE TREES	232
169. PATRIOTISM OF THE FROGS	233
170. THE ANT-LION	234
171. THE KING, THE DOG, AND THE SHADOW	235
172. THE DRAGONFLY AND THE BEE	237
173. THE AGING LION AND THE FOX	238
174. THE CROW AND THE SWAN	239
175. THE YOUNG BULLS AND THE LION	240
176. THE MONKEYS BUILDING A CITY	242
177. THE MOON AND THE SUN	243
178. THE EAGLE, THE PARTRIDGE AND THE ANT	244
179. THE EAGLE AND THE OWL	245
180. THE ROOSTER, THE FOX AND THE DOG	246
181. THE BIRDCATCHER AND THE FALCON	248
182. THE CRANE - THE KING OF BIRDS	249
183. THE FOX AND THE STORK	250
184. THE SNAKE AND THE FARMER	251

185. THE WISE JUDGE	252
186. MISADVENTURES OF THE WOLF	255
187. THE WOLF, THE FOX AND THE MULE	257
188. SHAH ABBAS, THE JUG OF WINE AND THE MIDDLEMAN	258
189. THE WEALTHY MAN AND HIS TWO SONS	260
190. THE KING OF BABYLON AND THE OLD MAN	263
191. THE SEA FROGS	264
192. THE LION, THE BEAR, AND THE WOLF	265
193. THE REPENTANT WOLF	266
194. THE WISE JUDGE	268
195. WINE	269
196. THE KING AND THE SNAKE	270
197. THE FOOL AND THE WATERMELON	271
198. THE FATHER AND THE SON	272
199. THE RULER AND THE WISE MAN	274
200. THE MOUSE AND THE CAMEL	275
201. TWO ARTISTS	276
202. THE WISHES OF THREE PRINCES	277
203. THE STORY OF THE GOATS AND THE WOLVES	278
204. THE FOX AND ST. GEORGE	280
205. DREAM INTERPRETATION	281
M1. THE KING AND THE RUNNING SERVANT	284
M2. THE SQUIRREL AND THE WOODPECKER	286
M3. THE PLUM TREE	287
M4. TWO FRIENDS	288
M5. THE BOWMAN AND THE DOCTOR	289
M6. THE SPRUCE AND THE MAGNOLIA	290
M7. TWO FRIENDS	291
M8. THE PAPERWORK	292
M9. THE OLD WOMAN AND HER GOAT	293
M10. TALENT AND DILIGENCE	295
M11. THE NOTHING	297

A FEW WORDS

In bringing to you *Foxbook: Medieval & Contemporary Fables from Armenia*, we are delighted to introduce a collection of over 200 Armenian medieval and contemporary fables that are being published by Dudukhouse for the first time. Our journey in compiling this anthology has been a fascinating deep-dive into the rich tapestry of Armenian storytelling, meticulously weaving together narratives that have spanned centuries.

The core of our translations has been drawn from two seminal works on Armenian medieval fables: Hovsep Orbeli's *Басни Средневековой Армении*[1] and Nikolai Marr's *Сборники притчъ Вардана*[2]. But we didn't stop there. To ensure we included a broad array of intriguing fables, we extended our quest beyond these volumes and turned to a variety of original sources.

We have carefully cross-verified each fable with its original Armenian versions, ensuring the essence of the tales remain intact when they are rendered in English.

Many of these fables already included morals, which we have preserved in their original context. We acknowledge that some of these lessons might feel anachronistic today, yet we chose to retain them as they provide an invaluable glimpse into the medieval Armenian mind.

Where fables lacked explicit morals, and where resonant, we took the liberty to add our own interpretations, coined as

---

[1] *Parables of Medieval Armenia*, Hovsep Orbeli, 1956
[2] *Collections of Vardan's Parables*, N. Marr, 1899

'Modern Insights.' Despite the passage of eight centuries, we find that human nature has remained remarkably consistent, making these age-old tales still relevant and insightful.

For a handful of fables that remained unclear to us, we decided to leave the interpretation open to you, the reader. We believe in the power of individual interpretation and look forward to hearing the myriad ways these stories might resonate with you.

We envision the *Foxbook* to serve not just as a collection of fables, but as a meditative guide. Throughout the book, we have left space for you to jot down your thoughts and reflections. We hope you will take these pauses as opportunities to engage deeply with the narratives, drawing parallels to your own life and learning from these timeless stories.

As a bonus, we have included a section of contemporary fables towards the end of the book. These narratives, penned by the translator and editor of this volume, were inspired by the wisdom of the medieval authors, as well as by tales heard growing up in Armenia and shared by mentors and older friends.

Lastly, in keeping with the spirit of interactive reading, we have *hidden a riddle* within these pages. Solve it, and you will uncover a final moral waiting to be discovered.

It is our hope that you will relish the fabulous journey into the world of Armenian fables as much as we have enjoyed translating and curating this book for you.

Enjoy the journey,
Sar Kamler

TRACING THE ROOTS:
A BRIEF HISTORY OF ARMENIAN FABLES

The *Foxbook*[3], a title that has resonated through the annals of Armenian literature, represents a venerable and remarkable tradition of fables that have been woven into the fabric of Armenian culture. These collections of tales, filled with wisdom and sagacity, have long captured the imagination of Armenian readership and beyond.

The fables found in this anthology give readers an opportunity to gain insight into the unique cultural and historical traditions of Armenia. With their moral and ethical teachings, these fables offer a valuable guide to correct common human vices and flaws, including hypocrisy, deception, theft, and self-interest. These lessons are conveyed through the use of animal, floral and human characters that are relatable, engaging, and universal. They represent a timeless form of storytelling that has influenced literature and storytelling across time and geography.

Armenian fables have origins that stretch back to time immemorial, predating even the invention of the Armenian alphabet in the fifth century A.D. The storytelling traditions received a significant boost with the introduction of Aesop's fables, as early as the 7th century. Nikolai Marr, a prominent Russian scholar, highlights in his *Collections of Vardan's Parables* that Armenian historians often referred to plots similar to Aesop's fables, even though these references didn't directly

---

[3] «Աղվեսագիրք», or «Աղուէսագիրք» | Foxbook

attribute the tales to Aesop himself[4]. Around the same period, another 15 fables, often referred to as *Olympian*, appeared in written form. These fables, assumed to be adapted from Greek rhetorical texts, served as a sort of revision to Aesop's works, although the origins of the "Olympian" label remain unclear. Furthermore, *The Physiologus*[5], an anonymous anthology offering moral teachings through animal characters, also became a part of the Armenian fable collection of that era[6].

Aesop's fables, which gained popularity in Armenia, became the dominant form of allegorical literature until the 12th century. The first comprehensive collection of the *Olympian fables*, however, was published only in 1842 by the Armenian Mekhitarist Congregation of Venice, alongside the fables of Mkhitar Gosh. This edition formed the foundation for W.Rothy's German translation in 1862, known as *Fabeln Des Olympianis, aus dem Armenischen*.

While the tradition of orally transmitting these tales was prevalent, it wasn't until the 12th century that the genre of fable in Armenian literature started to take definitive shape. This transformation can be credited to two eminent Armenian scholars, Mkhitar Gosh and Vardan Aygektsi, who played instrumental roles in advancing the fables as a literary form.

Mkhitar Gosh was a renowned Armenian philosopher, legislator, writer, and public figure born in the 1120s in the

---

[4] Марр, Н. Сборники притчъ Вардана. 1899. С. 433 | Marr, N. Collections of Vardan's Parables. 1899. P. 433.

[5] *The Physiologus (Բարոյախոս)* was a didactic Christian text, authored by an unknown writer in Greek. Originating from Alexandria and dating back to the 2nd to 4th century A.D., it provides moral lessons through the descriptions of animals, birds, and mythical creatures.

[6] Աբեղյան, Մանուկ. Հայոց միջնադարյան առակներն յեվ սոցիալական հարաբերությունները նրանց մեջ, էջ 8 | Abeghyan, M. Medieval Armenian Parables and Their Social Relationships. P. 8.

village of Gandzak, Artsakh. His life and wide-ranging activities are well-documented in various contemporary sources, the most notable of which are the accounts by 13th-century historian Kirakos of Gandzak. Gosh studied at his birthplace and was ordained as a celibate priest. He then went to Cilician Armenia, where he apprenticed to the famous priests of the Black Mountain monasteries and, upon returning to Armenia, founded a number of schools. He finally settled in the Getik monastery, where he built the New Getik monastery with the help of the Zakarian princes.

Gosh was highly respected among politicians and statesmen, participating in church meetings of Lori and Ani and serving as the confessor and advisor of Zakare II[7]. He was honored by his contemporaries and later generations with names like Wise and Meek Man, or Great Teacher[8].

Gosh's "Book of Judgment" is one of the greatest achievements of Armenian legal thought and consists of an introduction and the judgment book itself, with 251 articles. He strove to create a national code that would satisfy the legal demands of all classes of Armenian society and regulate their legal relations, protect national interests, and preserve the national identity in the fight against foreigners.

Gosh's collection of fables, consisting of 190 fables divided into three main sections, is also exceptional and valuable. The fables entered Armenian literature in the 12th century as a type of folk art, and Gosh compiled the collection for

---

[7] Zakare Zakaryan, also known as Zakaria II Mkhargrdzeli, was a prominent Armenian general in Queen Tamar of Georgia's army during the late 12th and early 13th centuries. He is notably recognized for his successful military campaigns and the establishment of significant religious structures in northern Armenia, such as the Harichavank and Akhtala Monasteries.

[8] *Մխիթար Գոշ.* Հայկական Սովետական Հանրագիտարան, հատոր 7, էջ 639 | *Mkhitar Gosh*, Armenian Soviet Encyclopedia, vol. 7, p. 630.

educational purposes. The fables discussed social and household problems, relationships between classes and individuals, extolling virtue and ridiculing shortcomings, stupidity, and ignorance.

Whenever the topic of Armenian fables arises, the name of Vardan Aygektsi is frequently mentioned alongside Mkhitar Gosh's name. This distinguished Armenian priest and writer who thrived during the 12th and 13th centuries is often seen as the torchbearer of Mkhitar Gosh's fable legacy. Born in the village of Maratha in the Armenian Kingdom of Cilicia, Aygektsi studied at the Arkakaghin Monastery of the Black Mountains, where he was eventually ordained as a priest. He preached in various places and participated in the coronation of Levon II, the King of Cilicia, in 1198. He was also persecuted and forced to leave his monastery in 1208, and later lived and worked at the Aygek monastery until his death.

Aygektsi wrote many speeches, papers, and sermons, and compiled a collection of testimonies called "The Root of Faith." He fought against Chalcedonianism, advocated for the integrity of the Armenian people, exposed human vices in his teachings, and defended the rights of the ordinary people. He tried to contribute to the strengthening of the fighting spirit of the Armenian people, encouraging them to work hard and fight for what they believed in.

Vardan was the first to introduce parables in his speeches and sermons, enhancing their effectiveness and understandability for his audience. His fables often featured the fox as the main character. Employing sharp satire, Aygektsi mocked corrupt judges, lawless clergymen, and worldly masters. Vardan's innovative approach brought a new literary genre into Armenian literature, which ultimately led to the formation of the *Foxbook*, a comprehensive collection of Armenian fables.

According to the *Armenian Soviet Encyclopedia*, Vardan Aygektsy primarily drew upon Aesop's fables and *The Physiologus* for his discourses. Of the known 60 Aesop's fables, Vardan utilized 13. He tailored their original civil morals to more spiritual ones and incorporated an additional 8 from *The Physiologus*. Given the popularity of these adapted fables, it is believed that he subsequently extracted these tales from his speeches and formed a few small collections[9].

Vardan Aygektsi's captivating style of storytelling triggered a wave of creating fable collections among his peers, with his works forming the core of many. These collections not only carried forward Vardan's fables but also introduced new tales and stories, fueling their evolution and expansion over time. Moreover, Vardan's adaptations gained such popularity that they eventually replaced or assimilated Aesop's fables in the Armenian literary canon.

Building on Vardan Aygektsi's storytelling legacy, numerous fable collections bearing the label of Vardan's Fables, proliferated over time. Many of them no longer bore any direct connection to Vardan Aygektsi himself. Occasionally, these collections merged into larger anthologies, with some hosting more than a hundred fables. The most notable anthology to emerge from this amalgamation was the *Foxbook*, so named for the recurring central character in many of its fables. This compilation marked a critical milestone in the evolution of Armenian fables, a testimony to the expanding genre and its widespread acceptance.

The physical manifestation of the *Foxbook* as we know it today came about in the 17th century, marking a pivotal moment in its history. It first saw publication in Amsterdam in 1668, home to a significant Armenian colony and an outstanding printing house. Later editions were released in Marseille in 1683

---

[9] Վարդան Այգեկցի. Հայկական Սովետական Հանրագիտարան, հատոր 11, էջ 310 | *Vardan Aygektsi*, Armenian Soviet Encyclopedia, vol. 11, p. 310.

and Livorno in 1698. As Hovsep Orbeli points out, these editions enjoyed extraordinary distribution and were repeatedly published, solidifying their place in Armenian literary tradition[10].

The *Foxbook* not only became a significant part of Armenian literature but also extended its influence beyond Armenia. Translations of the book appeared in many other languages, spreading the tales, their wisdom, and teachings beyond the Armenian borders. Despite changes in content and interpretation over the centuries, the *Foxbook* and the fable collections it represents continue to be an integral part of Armenian culture and literature, with many stories still living on in oral transmission today.

This newly minted edition of the *Foxbook: Medieval & Contemporary Fables from Armenia* that you now hold in your hands, marks a notable event, as it celebrates almost 355 years since its first publication in Amsterdam. This remarkable collection of Armenian fables, preserved through the generations, provides a rich exploration into Armenian history and culture.

In line with tradition, we have infused the collection with modern stories of our own creation, in the hopes that they will inspire you to come up with your unique tales. In this way, the *Foxbook* may evolve into a universal treasury of timeless stories.

These enduring fables serve as a poignant reminder of storytelling's value, with timeless lessons that remain pertinent even in our contemporary world. It's with immense pride that we share this anthology with you. We eagerly anticipate the enjoyment these narratives will bring, and the sharing of these stories for many more generations.

---

[10] Орбели, Иосиф. Басни средневековой Армении. Стр. 10. | Orbeli, Iosif. Fables of Medieval Armenia. p. 10.

ԳԻՐՔ
ԱՂՒԵՍԱՑ
ԵՒ
ԱՌԱՍՊԵԼԱԲԱՆ
ՆՈՒԹԵԱՆՑ.
Որէ
ԱՂՈՒԷՍԱԳԻՐՔ։
Ի Հայրապետութէ Տեառն
Յակոբայ Կաթուղիկոսի
Սրբոյ Էջմիածնի։
Յամբեղոտամումի
Ի Թուոյ Փրկչէն 1668։
Եւ Հայոց ռճժէ. Հոկտեմբերի
ամսոյ մէկ։

The Foxbook: Title Page from the Inaugural Edition,
Amsterdam, 1688

MEDIEVAL FABLES

1
A DROP OF HONEY
Vardan Aygektsi

A man had a store and he sold honey. A drop of honey fell to the ground and a wasp sat on it. A cat came and caught the wasp, and a dog chased after the cat, and the store owner hit the dog and killed it. Nearby there was another village, and the dog was from that village. When the dog's owner found out that the store owner killed his dog, he came and killed the store owner. The villagers from both villages then began a great war, and there was such a battle that only one person was left alive. And all of this was because of one drop of honey.

Original moral
The fable shows that everyone who lives in this world, like the people of these two villages, are fighting each other for just one drop of honey.

Modern Insight
Sometimes, small and insignificant actions can turn into unforeseen and devastating consequences. Be mindful of your actions and consider the potential outcome before making decisions. Do not let emotions or impulsivity control your behavior, or else it might lead to a potential conflict.

2
THE OX AND THE HORSE
Vardan Aygektsi

The ox and the horse were talking to each other. The horse asked, "Who are you, and what are you good for? I am a horse, and I am decorated with gold and silver by kings, princes, and barons who ride me." The ox replied, "I am the backbone of the whole country. I work, suffer, and exhaust myself, and in turn, you and your king consume my earnings, along with everyone else. If I stop working, then you and your king will perish immediately. Don't be ungrateful."

Original moral
This fable shows that there are people who work like an ox, and there are people who constantly ride and bring devastation to the country. Without the hard work of the ox, the horse and his rider would perish.

Modern Insight
In society, every individual has a crucial role to play, regardless of their status or how others perceive them. Recognize your worth and appreciate the effort you put in, even if it goes unrecognized or undervalued by others. Remember that everyone has a part to play, and each part is essential for the smooth functioning of the society.

3
THE BUFFALO
Mkhitar Gosh

The buffalo, while wallowing, beats the ground with its horns and loses them, and when they grow back, it no longer digs the soil with them.

Original moral
This fable highlights the wisdom of those who, having been once taught, reduce excesses of passion.

Modern Insight
Experience is a great teacher. Mistakes often hold important lessons that help us grow and improve. Reflect on your mistakes and learn from them, but even more crucially, learn from the mistakes of others around you.

4
THE CHICKEN AND THE MASTER
Mkhitar Gosh

A chicken, being caught by its owner, screamed very loudly, and those who heard her cry scolded her, "Why are you screaming for no reason?" And the chicken said, "I am scared because he does not always catch the chicken with good intentions. Sometimes, hanging them upside down, he carries them for many days, and sometimes he even roasts them on coals and eats them."

Modern Insight
It's easy to judge others without knowing their circumstances. Take time to understand the people around you and enjoy harmonious relationships blossoming around. Practice empathy and treat others with kindness and respect, even if you don't agree with their point of view.

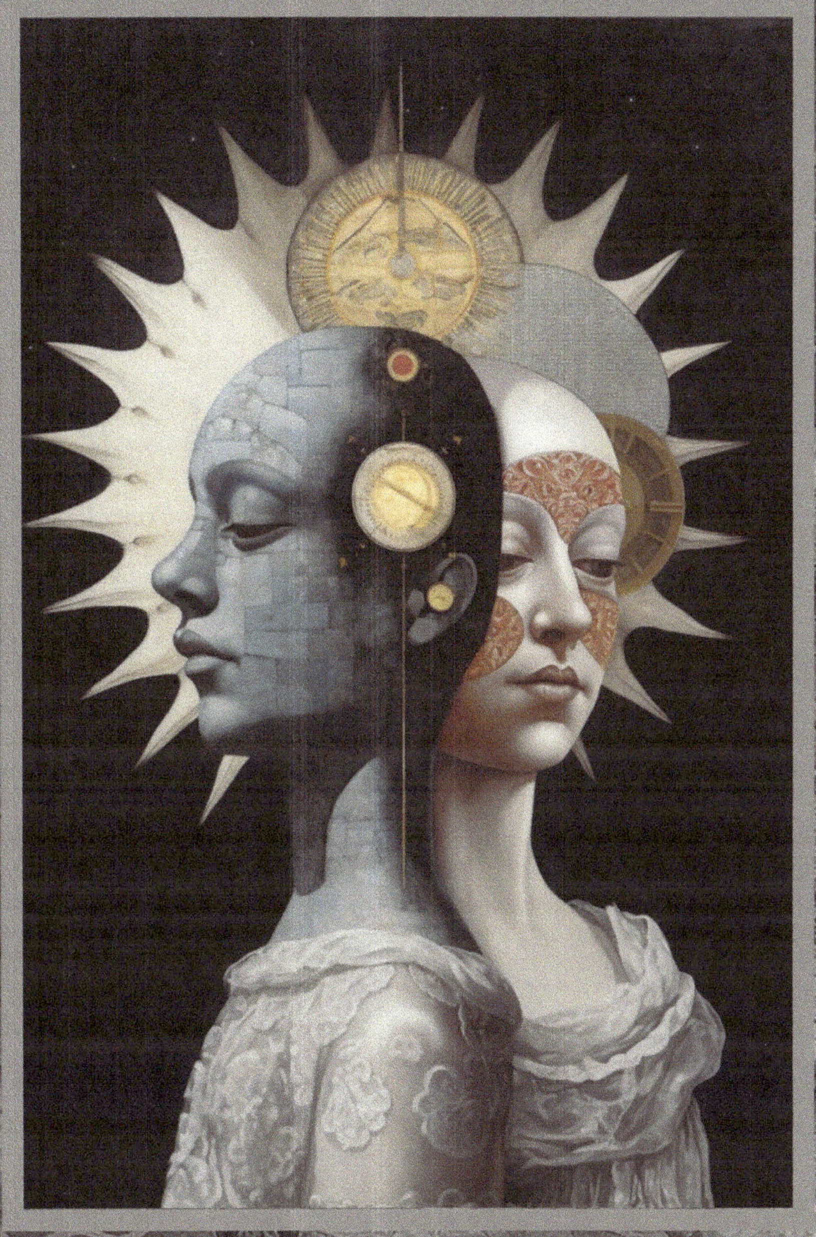

5
THE CHEETAH
Mkhitar Gosh

The cheetah, having failed to catch its prey, blamed the leader of its pack and then refused to eat, drink, or ride on horseback. The leader replied, "You have only yourself to blame, for you chased the game lazily, without determination."

Original moral
This fable is a critique of laziness, as those who put in minimal effort either spiritually or physically and fail to achieve success tend to complain rather than accept responsibility for their actions.

Modern Insight
Take full responsibility for your own actions whatever the results might be. Blaming others for your failures, laziness and lack of determination is a proven course to failure. Work hard and be persistent in your pursuits to stand on the top of the hill.

6
THE CHURCH AND THE MILL
Vardan Aygektsi

The church, proud of its holiness, said, "I am the temple and the house of God. In me, priests and parishioners come to pray to God and perform liturgies, and God reconciles with the world and forgives sins!" Then the mill spoke up and responded, "What you say is true and correct, but do not forget my merits: I work day and night to earn a living so that the priests and parishioners can eat and then come to you to pray and worship God."

Original moral
This fable shows that there are people in the world who constantly work and labor like bees, while kings, princes, priests, and parishioners eat their earnings, and then go to church and bless and remember God.

7
THE WISE MAN AND THE TREES
Mkhitar Gosh

The wise man asked the trees, "Why is it that the more you grow upward, the deeper you send your roots?" They replied, "How can you, a thinker, not know that we could not bear so many branches and resist the pressure of the wind if we did not send deep branching roots? See our brothers, the beech and the pine: they may not be branchy, but without deep roots, they cannot resist the wind."

Original Moral

To grasp the true essence of things, whether in the physical or spiritual realm, it is crucial to establish a solid foundation. This will prevent stumbling during times of trial and enable one to do meaningful work. Conversely, if one starts superficially without delving deeper, they run the risk of being easily overturned.

8
THE ANT
Mkhitar Gosh

The ant is diligent in its work and very resourceful, but it completes its task with perseverance and patience.

Original Moral
Learn from this example: if you start a good deed, physical or spiritual, do not leave it unfinished.

9
THE PARTRIDGE AND THE HUNTER
Vardan Aygektsi

Hunter caught a partridge and wanted to kill her. The partridge cried and said, "Don't cut me, I will bring you many chicks and I will give them to your will." And hunter says to her, "You will die now from my hand because you want to betray your close ones and your tribe to death."

Modern Insight
Betrayal to benefit is short-lived. Even in difficult situations, hold onto your values and maintain your integrity to create lasting bonds. True success in any relationship, whether personal or professional, is built on a foundation of trust and loyalty.

10
THE DONKEY IN LION'S SKIN
Olympian

A donkey once disguised itself as a lion by wearing a lion's skin. From a distance, it even intimidated and caused a herd of cows and a flock of sheep to flee. However, when a strong wind blew and uncovered the donkey's deceit, everyone turned against him. He was exposed for who he truly was - a donkey pretending to be a lion.

Original Moral
As for you, the thinker, you deserve punishment. You are an ignoramus who pretends to be a scholar.

11
THE DOCTOR FROG
Vardan Aygektsi

The frog got a stethoscope and a jar of ointment and went around saying, "I am a doctor, a scientist, and I know the cure for all illnesses." So all the animals gathered to receive treatment. The fox came and, seeing this doctor, said, "You are covered in warts and pimples from head to toe, yet you treat others."

Original Moral
So is the person who, ignoring their own flaws, tries to instruct others.

Take a break for a moment.

You've journeyed through a tapestry of fables by now. Did any of them strike a chord within you? Did you recognize any situations, any threads of familiarity woven into these stories? This is your chance to let your thoughts flow. Grab the nearest pencil, and allow the space below to catch your cascading ideas...

_____

_____

_____

_____

_____

_____

_____

_____

_____

_____

_____

12
GOD AND HIS CREATIONS
Mkhitar Gosh

When God was crafting his creations, he was wary of any single entity gaining supremacy. Thus, he mixed the heavy with the light, the weak with the strong, so that if any opposition arose, it would be between themselves and not against their creator. This fable teaches monarchs to set large and small against each other, so that they fight among themselves and not against the kings.

13
THE FALCON AND THE PARTRIDGE
Mkhitar Gosh

The falcon congratulated the partridge upon seeing her with many children and praised God. The partridge replied, "If you truly give praise to God, then be blessed yourself." The falcon then attacked one of her chicks and snatched it. The partridge said, "Now it is clear that you were only praising God out of greed."

Original Moral
This fable reveals the nature of princes, as they take pleasure in the successes of those under their power, considering their possessions to be their own rather than belonging to the rightful owner.

14
DOVE'S MEEKNESS
Mkhitar Gosh

Someone frequently took chicks from a dove's nest and praised the dove for its meekness. And the dove said, "Oh, you ruthless one, if I am called meek, then is it permissible for you to be bloodthirsty? Here it is clear that you are scheming, praising me."

Original Moral
The fable criticizes the habits of aggressors (offenders): knowing that virtuous people are not vengeful, they become even angrier and praise the behavior of the oppressed.

15
WISE CROWS
Vardan Aygektsi

A crow gathered her young and taught them, saying, "My children, be careful, beware of man and especially when he leans down to pick up a rock." The young crows asked, "Mother, what should we do if the man has already picked up the rock in advance?" The mother replied, "Well, now I know that you won't be caught."

Modern Insight
Thinking ahead, staying vigilant and anticipating potential dangers can prepare you for any situation.

16
THE HAWKS AND THE EAGLES
Mkhitar Gosh

The hawks said to their parents, "Why don't you catch us live prey like the eagles and falcons do? Instead, you bring us the bones of dead animals!" And they said, "Children, that's why God made us long-lived, so that we don't kill the living and are content with the dead, like priests, and not plunder the living, like princes."

Original Moral
This fable wishes that we live off the rightful and fair inheritance of the deceased, rather than unlawfully taking from the living; thus, we will become eternal on earth.

17
THE WOLF AND THE LAMB
Vardan Aygektsi

There was a beautiful lamb in the pen. The wolf climbed in and grabbed it to eat. The lamb fell at his feet and said, "God has given me to you, so have mercy on me and first play on your trumpet, so that I can listen and my wish will come true; for I have heard from my fathers that the wolf kind are great trumpet players." The wolf believed these foolish words, sat down and blew his trumpet with all his might, and the dogs woke up and attacked him. He ran away, sat on a hill, cried and beat himself up saying, "I deserve this punishment: who made me a trumpet player, when I have always been a butcher and the son of a butcher?"

Original Moral
This fable shows that many wise people are deceived and believe nonsense like the wolf, then regret it; many take on a task that is not suitable for them and end up in trouble.

18
SPIDER
Vardan Aygektsi

A spider naturally spins webs to hunt, but sometimes it spins so much that it gets sick and dies. And the fruit of its labor is just a fly.

Original Moral
So it's the same with greedy people: they lose their souls by accumulating the wealth of this world, which, compared to the kingdom of heaven, is like just a single fly.

19
THE WOLF AND THE DONKEY
Vardan Aygektsi

The wolf found a fat donkey and wanted to eat it. The donkey said, "I beg you, oh wolf, since God has delivered me to you for sustenance, eat me, but first heal the sore of my heart: a nail has painfully pierced my leg and is tormenting me." The wolf approached the donkey from behind to pull out the nail, but the donkey fiercely lay down and hit the wolf in the muzzle, and his jaw was shattered. The wolf sadly cried and said, "Justly do I bear this misfortune, for from the beginning and always I have been a butcher, so who then made me a farrier[6]?"

Original Moral
This fable shows that many people regret and lament having gotten involved in a business or trade they didn't learn and that doesn't bring them benefit at the right time.

---

[6] A farrier is a professional who specializes in the care and maintenance of horses' hooves, including trimming, shoeing, and treating various hoof-related conditions.

20
A MAN AND GARLIC
Mkhitar Gosh

Galen[7] referred to garlic as a peasant's theriak[8]. One man, having heard this, ate a whole measure of it and, becoming delirious, went blind.

Original Moral
The meaning of this fable is that wise men say that fear can cure, but if the measure is exceeded recklessly, people will become spiritually blind.

---

[7] Galen (Aelius Galenus or Claudius Galenus) was a Greek physician who lived in the Roman Empire during the 2nd century AD. He was one of the most influential figures in the development of Western medicine and was considered a prominent physician, surgeon, and philosopher in his time.

[8] Theriac was an antidote and a cure for all diseases.

21
THE CRIPPLED LION
Mkhitar Gosh

The lion, having broken his leg, complained to all the animals, "You are my subjects, for I am the ruler of beasts, why are you not now bringing sacrifices for me so that I may recover?" And they said, "Because we have not found protection from you from the bear, the wolf, or other beasts, and you have not shown mercy to us. But it is fitting for us to offer gifts to God for sending you such misfortune."

Modern Insight
Loyalty and respect must be earned and cannot be inherited or acquired instantly. Treat others with kindness, respect and fairness to build long-lasting support and loyalty.

22
THE OX
Mkhitar Gosh

An ox ran away from the plow's yoke, and being caught by the plowman, was brought to the threshing floor. Escaping from there, he was harnessed to a carriage, but managed to break free again. However, he was captured and used for various tasks. Eventually, he realized that escape was impossible and reconciled himself to his situation, no longer attempting to run away.

Original Moral
For those who wish to spend their time in idleness and without purpose, a piece of advice: constantly change tasks until you find one that suits you. Being idle in society is impossible.

23
THE LIONESS AND THE FOX
Vardan Aygektsi

The lioness gave birth to a lion cub, and all the animals gathered to see it and take part in the celebration. The fox came and during the celebration, in the midst of all this gathering, loudly scolded the lioness and mocked her, "Is this your power, that you give birth to only one offspring, not many?" The lioness calmly replied, "Yes, I give birth to one offspring, but I give birth to lions, not foxes like you."

Original Moral
This fable shows that it is better to have one man who does good before God than a thousand unrepentant sinners, and it is better to have one poor man who does not deserve hell than a thousand kings who do, and it is better to have one good son than a hundred wicked and evil sons.

Modern Insight
Excellence in a single task often outweighs mediocre performance in several.

24
ARAMAZD AND THE SNAKE
Vardan Aygektsi

Aramazd[9] was organizing the wedding of his son. All the animals came and brought gifts to the newlyweds. A snake came as well and gifted a beautiful, fragrant branch, a rose with leaves. But Aramazd chased away the snake and said, "It is not appropriate to accept anything from your mouth, full of poison."

Modern Insight
Exercise caution when accepting gifts from those who have a reputation for being untrustworthy, as their intentions may not be genuine.

---

[9] Aramazd was the chief and creator god in the Armenian version of Zoroastrianism. He was regarded as a generous god of fertility, rain, and abundance, as well as the father of the other gods, including Anahit, Mihr, and Nané.

25
THE CAMEL, THE WOLF, AND THE FOX
Vardan Aygektsi

A camel, wolf, and fox went together and, finding a white loaf left by travelers, said, "What shall we do with it, since it is not enough for us all?" The fox said, "It's food for one; whoever among us is older and more worn out, let him eat." And all three agreed. The wolf said, "I am the wolf that Noah took in the ark during the flood." The fox said, "You are a friend to my grandson, for I am the fox that God created and presented to Adam, and he called me a fox." But the camel stretched his neck, took the loaf, raised his head, began to chew and said, "You guys are short, and you talk like that! Well, what about these legs of mine, have they grown on a suckling?" The wolf and the fox walked around but could not harm him, so they left him alone and ran away.

Original Moral
Those who are physically stronger or in a position of power can take what they want without regard for others even if it means breaking a previously agreed-upon arrangement. The weaker may complain or try to resist, but they may ultimately be unable to do anything about it. Staying wise and being able to adapt to changing circumstances might be the only choice in these cases.

26
THE LION, THE WOLF AND THE FOX
Vardan Aygektsi

The lion, the wolf, and the fox went hunting and found a ram, a sheep, and a lamb. The lion said to the wolf, testing him, "Divide these animals between us." And the wolf said, "Oh king, it was God who divided them: the ram for you, the sheep for me, and the lamb for the fox." The lion became angry, gave the wolf a slap and his eyes popped out, and, sitting down, he cried bitterly. And the lion said to the fox, "Divide these animals between us." The fox said, "Oh king, it was God who divided them: the ram for your lunch, the sheep for your breakfast, and the lamb for your dinner." And the lion asked, "Oh miserable trickster, who taught you this fair division?" The fox said, "The eyes of the wolf that popped out, taught me."

Original Moral
The fable shows that many villains learn and stop their evil doings when rulers and princes hang thieves and the wicked.

27
THE SUNFLOWER
Mkhitar Gosh

The flower of the reed and those like it were accused of being sun worshipers. But it, raising its arms to the sun, swore by the sun, "I am not a sun worshiper!"

Original Moral
This fable exposes those who, being accused of a blatant vice and trying to hide it, thus make themselves more exposed than they manage to conceal.

28
THE WIDOW AND THE PRIEST
Vardan Aygektsi

The priest stole a cow from the widow and put it in the barn. The widow found out and said to the priest, "Father, the time of my death has come, let's go to the barn so that I can confess." Then the priest transferred the cow inside, then - in the altar[10], and from there - to the church. And the widow said to him, "Father, the deathbed confession should be made in front of the altar." The priest lifted the cow to the altar and closed the veil[11]. Entering the church, the widow lifted the curtain and said to the cow, "O wicked one, I always considered you a cow, so tell me, who put you to serve Mass?"

Modern Insight
Dishonesty and greed can lead to one's downfall. Find a clever way to show that deceitful behavior can never be truly hidden.

---

[10] An altar is a raised structure, typically a table or stand, used for worship or offering in various religious traditions. It is often the central focus of religious ceremonies or rituals.

[11] Veil - a large veil on the altar platform of Armenian churches, which is moved to the right side for the viewer and hides the altar and the priest standing in front of it from the worshippers on certain days and moments of worship.

29
THE BEAR AND THE ANT
Mkhitar Gosh

The bear, using its paw, tore apart an ant hill, licked the ants, and ate them. The ant, seeking revenge, asked the wasp, hornet, mosquito, tick, fly, and other insects to help him. They stung the bear in its eyes and ears, causing him to roar in pain and run away. In its agony, the bear hit its head against rocks, resulting in deep cuts, and the insects further attacked it. Even the small fish entered its stomach and caused pain. The bear, trying to escape, jumped into the water but drowned due to its wounds.

Original Moral
The moral of this fable is that the strong should not underestimate the weak, as the small can be strengthened by their wisdom to defeat the mighty. Therefore, it is wise to fear the small just as much as the great.

30
THE DYING CAMEL
Vardan Aygektsi

A fox came across a dying camel and sat down nearby. The camel asked, "Why did you come here?" The fox said, "You are going to die, and I will eat the meat." The camel said, "Oh, poor fox, you cannot wait for me to die, for my neck is long and my soul will slowly leave." And the fox responded, "But I, like all of my kind, am very patient; I will wait, even if you take forty days."

Modern Insight
Patience is a virtue that will lead to success. Work towards your goals with patience and persistence and the reward will be eventually yours.

31
THE HOOPOE
Mkhitar Gosh

The hoopoe, despite his admirable trait of caring for his elderly father, was often criticized for his bad smell. In an attempt to mask it, he found a fragrant substance and placed it on his chest. However, the scent did not conceal his stench.

Original Moral
The fable addresses those who, although deserving praise for many things, cannot hide one inherent flaw despite their efforts.

32
THE HEDGEHOG AND THE HAMSTER
Mkhitar Gosh

The hamster convinced the hedgehog, "I will take your son for upbringing, and we will be friends." And when the hedgehog, after long persuasion, agreed, the hamster said, "It's difficult to kiss him, so take off the needles from him, so I can pet him." And, yielding to deception, the hedgehog did this, and when he gave his son to the hamster, the latter ate the hedgehog, and nothing could be done, and the hedgehog went away in great sorrow.

Modern Insight
Always be careful when making deals and trusting deceitful people who may take advantage of your trust and harm you. Keep your defenses up and never give up your tools of protection.

33
THE TURNIP AND THE CARROT
Mkhitar Gosh

Turnip asked the carrot, "Why do you bury yourself so deep in the ground?" And the carrot replied, "I am amazed at your boldness, for being red and white, you expose yourself on display!" To which the turnip replied, "That's bad, but your cowardice is also bad!"

Original Moral
The fable urges us to reside somewhere in the middle between fear and daring, for both are evil.

34
THE OWL AND THE EAGLE
Mkhitar Gosh

The owl sent a messenger to the eagle, asking for his daughter as a bride and saying, "You are the day's knight, and I am the night's warrior. It's worthy for our families to be united." After much persuasion, the eagle agreed to the marriage proposal. And when the wedding took place, during the day the groom could not see the light, and the guests laughed at him, and when night came, the bride could not see anything, and again the guests ridiculed them. As a result, the wedding was immediately called off.

Modern Insight
Before committing to any partnership or alliance, carefully consider whether the parties involved are truly compatible in their values, goals, and abilities. Mismatched pairs often lead to disappointment and failure.

35
THE FALCON AND THE DOVE
Mkhitar Gosh

The falcon chased after a dove, and the dove cried out, "I am a gift to the Lord, do not harm me!" But the falcon replied, "A gift to the Lord should be on the Lord's throne, not flying around here in the air!" And with that, he caught and ate the dove.

36
THE EAGLE
Mkhitar Gosh

All the birds under the Eagle's rule asked him, "We will respectfully provide you with food, but please do not harm us if something happens." He agreed and for a long time, they lived in peace. But the birds began to mock the Eagle and even plotted to overthrow him. The Sparrow boasted, "I will blind him by defecating in his eyes." Others also bragged about their abilities and even fought with the Eagle. He could not tolerate it and attacked, killing many of them.

Original Moral
This fable illustrates the actions of a just and faithful ruler, and those who lack faith: despite the peaceful life he provides, they rise up without reason and mock him, even going to war. Reluctantly, the ruler must bring them to justice and show no mercy.

37
THE MERLIN AND THE RINGDOVE
Mkhitar Gosh

The ringdove's chick escaped from the claws of the merlin. And the merlin said, "Let this be a gift to God." The ringdove laughed at him, "The only thing that can be a gift to God is what you present with your own hands."

Original Moral
This fable depicts the behavior of a shepherd who calls the loss of sheep to predators or wolves a gift from the lord.

38
THE BUFFALO - SURVEYOR
Mkhitar Gosh

The buffalo desired to become a land surveyor. But he grew tired of measuring, so he went and lay down in the reeds. His teacher scolded him for being lazy, but he replied, "Is it only the land that needs to be measured? I will become a water surveyor".

Original Moral
This fable applies to those who, after leaving behind bad behavior, return to their old habits and, when exposed, say "Are there only the righteous ones? There are also sinners."

Modern Insight
Regardless of the path chosen, obstacles are inevitable. Success is not about avoiding challenges, but persisting through them with dedication and resilience. Laziness and lack of persistence only lead to a cycle of unfulfilled ambitions.

39
THE FOOL AND THE DOCTOR
Mkhitar Gosh

Galen was once teaching about physical health, saying, "Those who are careful with their food and drink will not need our skill." Someone, hearing this, neither ate nor drank and as a result, fell ill and began to blame Galen. Upon hearing this, Galen said, "Don't you know that we are helpers, not creators of nature? Why didn't you understand my words and act accordingly?"

Original Moral
This example shows that it is necessary to listen carefully to mentors and doctors and to act accordingly to achieve spiritual health. One should also avoid excess and self-restriction, as both can lead to harm.

40
THE WOLF AND THE SHEEP
Vardan Aygektsi

The wolf came up to a mountain and saw a flock of sheep at the foot of the hill, and said "Peace be upon you!" But the oldest ram said to his companions, "Brothers, although he wishes us peace, run for your life, whoever and however we can!"

Modern Insight
Do not trust the words of those who have caused harm in the past. Be vigilant and act wisely to protect yourself from potential danger.

*Your mind, a sponge, has soaked up wisdom,
Go get your pen, then give it freedom.*

41
THE THIEF
Mkhitar Gosh

The thief climbed into a wealthy house, but was caught in the act by the owner. The owner attempted to beat him with a stick, but the thief managed to overpower him and beat him instead. The thief then asked the owner, "Why, upon seeing me at work, did you not say: 'God help'?" The owner shouted for help and brought the thief to court. When the judge asked the thief, "In what good deeds did you ask for blessings?" The thief replied, "In whatever I was doing. If it was not good for him, then it was good for me." However, his response did not help him at all, and he was ultimately sentenced to death by hanging.

Original Moral
This fable serves as a warning against the tendency of villains to rationalize their actions and consider themselves good, even when their actions cause harm to others. In the end, such individuals will face the consequences of their actions, both in this life and in the afterlife.

42
THE BEAR AND THE FOX
Vardan Aygektsi

The lion became ill and the animals rushed to tend to him. The fox was late, so the bear began to slander her to the lion, and her friends told the fox. The lion said, "You have come at a bad time, you trash. Tell me why you were late?" "Do not be angry, good king, for, I swear by you, worrying about your health, I visited many of the best doctors and found a remedy." And the lion asked, "Welcome, clever one, what is this remedy?" - "It is very affordable and useful! The doctors said, "Take the skin off the bear, and, still warm, put it on the lion, and the pain will immediately subside." The lion commanded, and they grabbed the bear and started to peel off his skin. He howled and raged. And the fox said, "Here you are, and to all who, entering the palace, will slander others."

Original Moral
This fable shows that it is not appropriate to gossip and condemn others. It is better to reflect on your actions and examine your shortcomings.

43
THE LION AND THE FOX
Vardan Aygektsi

The lion hired the fox and said, "When you see my eyes filled with blood, let me know. That's a sign that I am ready for the hunt." So the lion hunted, and both of them ate happily. Feeling proud, the fox left the lion, and hired the wolf. She said, "Whether my eyes are filled with blood or not, if I ask, say "Yes, there is a lot of blood in your eyes." And the fox asked as she learned from the lion, "Are my eyes filled with blood?", and the wolf said, "There is a lot of blood in your eyes, it's very thick[12]." The fox settled on the path, and the deer ran up. She rushed to meet them, as she learned from the lion. The deer kicked her with their feet, broke her skull, and she fell unconscious. And the wolf said, "Get up, now indeed the blood in your eyes has thickened."

Original Moral
This fable illustrates the danger of arrogance, as demonstrated by the fox. Being arrogant beyond one's means and abilities, whether in spiritual or physical matters, can lead to failure.

---

[12] Refers to the thickness of the blood in the eyes, indicating that the blood is very dense or viscous.

44
THE CONFESSION
Vardan Aygektsi

Someone went to the abbot and said, "I hit a spiritual leader." The abbot said, "Did you hit with a stick or a sword?" - "With a sword." He asked, "Did you hit with the flat side or the edge?" - "With the edge." He asked, "Did you wound or kill?" - "I killed!" The abbot said, "You scoundrel, after murder you talk about hitting? How much more severe is murder than a beating!"

45
THE MONKEY AND THE FISHERMAN
Vardan Aygektsi

The monkey had a habit of mimicking people's actions. She saw a fisherman cast his nets to catch fish and then go to eat. She descended from the tree, took the net, and tried to cast it like the fisherman, but got tangled in it and said, "I'm in trouble because I got involved in something I don't understand."

Original Moral
This fable teaches us not to undertake tasks we are unskilled in or that do not match our abilities, both physically and spiritually. Doing so will lead to loss without any benefit, and eventually, we will become nothing.

46
THE PRAYER OF THE WIDOW
Vardan Aygektsi

A widow had a cow, and her stepson had a donkey. The stepson would steal feed from the cow and give it to the donkey. So the widow prayed to God that the donkey would die, but the cow died instead. The widow cried and said, "Woe is me, my prayer has turned back on me! God, how could you not be able to tell the difference between a donkey and a cow?"

Original Moral
This fable shows: do not pray for evil to befall your companion, lest it befall to yourself.

47
THE WOLVES AND THE SHEEP
Olympian's Fables

The wolves sent a message to the sheep saying, "The reason for the constant wars and persistent disputes between us and you is the dogs because they irritate us and incite our hostility against you; but if they are removed, peace will come between you and us and there will be no more evil from us!" The sheep, being foolish, agreed and rejected the protection of the dogs, and the wolves, finding them without dogs, attacked and killed them all.

Original Moral
The fable teaches us to be wary of those who have a history of hostility and aggression towards us. We should not easily trust their promises of peace and goodwill, and instead keep our defenses up and remain cautious around them. It is important to recognize those who have a history of being deceitful or violent and not let our guard down, even if they make enticing promises.

48
THE WIDOW AND HER SON
Vardan Aygektsi

A widow had ten goats and her son always took them out to pasture. Every day, the mother would pour one cup of water into the milk, and then sell it. The son said, "Why are you sinning by pouring water into the milk?" She replied, "Son, we don't have much milk, so I do it so we can have more and have enough for the winter." One day, while the boy was out grazing the goats, a storm came. It rained heavily, a stream formed, and carried off the goats and drowned them in the river. The boy returned home alone with his stick. The mother asked, "Where are the goats? Why did you come back so early?" He replied, "Mother, those cups of water you poured into the milk came together, turned into a stream, and the stream caught our goats and carried them away in the river."

Modern Insight
The universe has a way of bringing everything back to a balance. Even small dishonest acts can eventually lead to unexpected consequences. Likewise, good deeds can have a positive ripple effect that may not be immediately apparent, but can ultimately bring balance and harmony to our lives. Be mindful of your actions and always strive to do what is right, even in small ways, as it can have a significant impact on your future.

49
THE HEIFERS AND THE BULLS
Vardan Aygektsi

The heifers were frolicking and criticizing the bulls, "You can't get rid of persecution and labor." And then the king came, and heifers were gathered and slaughtered for the king's lunch and his army. And the bulls said, "Look, children[13], for this day you have lived in idleness and fattened up."

Modern Insight
Those who are too comfortable in their current situation and mock others who work hard, may one day find themselves in a vulnerable position and regret not putting in the effort to prepare for the future. Hard work and preparation are important in order to avoid being caught off guard and facing the consequences of one's own negligence.

---

[13] Refers to heifers.

50
A TRADER'S PRAYER
Vardan Aygektsi

A man prayed to God to send him 100 drams[14], and said, "If you give me 100 drams, then I will give you ten for lamp oil[15]." And by God's will, one day, he found ninety drams and said, "God, my creator, it is very clever of you to have held onto your ten drams for oil, and then to give me 100 drams without them."

Modern Insight
People often will make promises in exchange for something. But often, when they get what they want, they will find ways not to fulfill them. It's important to remember our commitments and be true to our word.

---

[14] Dram was an Armenian coin or unit of weight equal to around 4 grams.
[15] Lamp oil is the oil that burns in lamps - fixtures, traditionally lit in front of icons.

51
THE DROWNING DONKEY
Vardan Aygektsi

The donkey fell into the river and began to drown, splashing water in fear. His manure floated to the surface and, swimming, overtook the ass. And the donkey cried out, "Ah, you scoundrel, rogue, you came out of my body, tell me, please, where did you learn to swim?"

Original Moral
It is very unworthy when young men teach the old men, ignoramuses - scholars, fools - wise men.

52
THE TRUSTING WOLF
Olympian's Fables

The babysitter threatened the crying child, "If you don't stop, I'll throw you to the wolf!" The wolf heard this and, in the hopes of the threat being carried out, waited until evening to take the baby. As evening came, the child fell asleep, and the wolf returned home empty-handed from the hunt. The wolf's mate asked him, and he explained, "I have believed a woman and was deceived!"

Original Moral
Don't trust! Know that they promise much for their own ulterior motives. Their disposition towards those who rely on them lasts only as long as their words are heard.

53
THE MOLE
Vardan Aygektsi

The mole, by nature, constantly digs the earth and does not stay anywhere for long. They say that it smells bad, and moves from place to place because of its scent, thinking it's from the location. So it digs tunnels here and there. But the smell is from itself.

Modern Insight
Don't attribute your problems or shortcomings to external factors. The root of the problem almost always lies within yourself. Unaware of our flaws or negative traits, we often try to escape or ignore them instead of addressing them. Look inward and work on improving yourself rather than looking outward for solutions to your problems.

54
THE BED OF A DEBTOR
Vardan Aygektsi

An elder in the imperial city of Constantinople was deeply in debt. No one knew about it, and he was not worried at all and slept carelessly. And when he died, it turned out that he was in debt all around. And the treasurer, having heard about this, said, "Bring me his bed, for it is miraculous and gives sleep to a man. It's amazing and worthy of admiration, how could he sleep with so much debt!"

Modern Insight
Living within one's means and avoiding excessive debt is important for financial stability and peace of mind. The modern society's reliance on debt to purchase major assets, such as homes and cars, has normalized the concept of carrying significant financial obligations. However, carrying too much debt can lead to financial stress and the inability to fulfill other obligations or pursue opportunities. It is essential to manage one's finances responsibly and avoid overspending. This may involve making difficult decisions and sacrifices, but it is necessary for long-term financial security.

55
THE FOX AND THE BAIT
Vardan Aygektsi

The fox saw a man scattering pieces of cheese on the road and asked him, "Why are you doing this?" The man replied, "I am doing it for the salvation of my soul." The fox said, "If you're scattering cheese for your soul, then blessed is your soul, but if it's for my hide, then woe to your soul."

Modern Insight
Be aware of the true intentions of others and avoid falling into their traps. Listen to your intuition, be mindful of your entourage, and remain vigilant in our interactions with others to avoid falling victim to their schemes.

56
THE DEER AND THE DOGS
Olympian's Fables

Mother said to the deer, "You are taller than the dogs, faster, and with longer horns to protect you. What happened to you that made you so afraid of dogs?" The deer replied, "I am well aware of my height and proud of my horns, and I can beat them in running, but as soon as I hear the bark, my thoughts get confused, I fall into terror and flee."

Original Moral
So, no comfort and encouragement strengthens the naturally timid.

57
THE ENVIOUS
Vardan Aygektsi

There was a king who knew that his warriors secretly envied each other. And the king said to one of them, "Ask me for any promotion you want, so that I may reward you, but with the provision that I will give your companion double what I give you." He thought to himself, "If I ask for any blessings, he will give it to my companion twice as much!" And he said to the king, "Pluck out one of my eyes!" So that the king would pluck out both of his companion's eyes.

Modern Insight

Envy is a powerful emotion that can cause you to act irrationally and make decisions that are not in your best interest. When envy takes control, it can create a never-ending cycle of competition, where you constantly try to one-up others in an effort to prove your worth. This type of behavior can lead to resentment, damage relationships, and distract you from achieving your goals. Recognize the harmful effects of envy and work to avoid letting it control your thoughts and actions. Instead, focus on your own strengths and accomplishments and celebrate the successes of others.

58
THE ROOSTERS
Vardan Aygektsi

Two roosters were fighting on the street, and one defeated the other. Exhilarated, the winner flew up, climbed onto a high rooftop, started strutting around, singing, and flapping his wings in celebration of his victory, proud of himself. But, suddenly, an eagle swooped down, grabbed him and carried him away to the sky.

Original Moral
Do not rejoice in the death of your enemy and boast about your victory.

59
PLATO AND THE BABY ELEPHANT
Mkhitar Gosh

An elephant sent his son to study philosophy with Plato. At first, Plato taught him to sit in the auditorium with his legs folded, but the baby elephant could not do it. He then ordered him to incline his head, but he wasn't successful at that as well. Plato returned him to his father and said, "Your son is more suited to be in a royal palace, always standing, rather than in my lecture hall, as he cannot sit or tilt his head."

Original Moral
This fable instructs us to choose for each position someone suitable in character and temperament and in similar matters.

60
THE GOAT AND THE WOLF
Vardan Aygektsi

Once a goat was sitting on a high wall, and a wolf came and sat under it. The goat looked at him and said, "Oh, I want to come down and butt this wolf's belly with my horns!" Then the wolf said, "I wish I could see the goat come and butt my belly with her horns!"

Original Moral
This fable shows how a foolish person, looking at himself, imagines that he can defeat the great and, when defeated, falls into their hands, and then his powerlessness is revealed.

61
THE ROOSTER AND THE KING
Vardan Aygektsi

A rooster was brought to the palace to sing at night. The king, seeing the rooster, said, "I will give you everything you need, but you have to stay clean in the palace." The king noticed that the rooster was always digging in the dirt with his feet and beak and said, "Fool, didn't I tell you to stay clean? But you're always digging in the dirt and making a mess in the palace." The rooster replied, "It's hard to give up your old ways."

Original Moral
Habitual traits are worse than inborn ones: an inborn trait can be suppressed, but it is difficult to change an acquired one.

62
THE YOUNG WOLF AND THE ALPHABET
Vardan Aygektsi

Once, a young wolf was caught and taught how to read letters. They said, "Say A", and he replied, "A lamb". They said, "Say B", and he said, "Bison". They said, "Say C", and he answered, "Caribou". They said, "Say D", and he said, "Deer". They said, "Say E", and he replied, "Excuse me, but if I don't hurry, the herd will get away, and I won't catch it[16]."

Modern Insight
Avoid teaching people who are firmly set in their ways. Focus on your own growth and development instead of trying to change the unchangeable.

---

[16] In the original story the young wolf is being taught the Armenian alphabet and chooses words for each letter that reflect his nature as a predator.

63
THE PIG AND THE KING
Vardan Aygektsi

A king, who was magnificent and well-intentioned, housed a beautiful pig in his palace and wished to exalt and glorify it. He made a golden ring worth one thousand dahekans[17] for her and put on her a priceless white silk robe embroidered with gold, and put the ring in her snout. But in the morning, she wandered through the city, dragging her robe and ring in the dirt.

Modern Insight
External decorations cannot change one's true nature or behavior. In fact, the shinier the appearance, the more likely there is an emptiness inside. Humans often use material things to disguise the emptiness they feel inside. Therefore, look beyond the external appearance and explore their internal world to truly understand who they are as a person. You may be surprised by what you discover.

---

[17] Dahekan is a unit of weight and a gold coin used in ancient Armenia, named after the Persian king Darius I the Great.

64
THE MAGPIE AND THE PRIEST
Mkhitar Gosh

The magpie gave his son to be trained as a priest. But the son always liked to whistle and caw. And the priest taught him to recite hymns and psalms, which leads to grief and repentance in the soul. But he became more and more playful, saying, "My father's art is a source of joy, but yours is a source of sorrow." And becoming deaf to his studies, he returned home.

Modern Insight
Trying to force someone to follow a path that does not suit their natural abilities and interests can lead to frustration and failure. Each individual possesses unique talents and inclinations. Recognize, support, and encourage these differences for their success and fulfillment.

65
THE ILL-TEMPERED CAMEL
Mkhitar Gosh

A driver struck a camel, and the camel angrily said, "Watch out, don't hit me when I am sad, or you'll die from me." The driver asked, "Please tell me, what are the signs of your sadness, so that, noticing them, I don't hit you?" And the camel said, "When you see that my lips are drooping and my legs are stubbornly silent, these are the signs of sadness." The driver replied, "But you're always like that. How can I know?"

Modern Insight
There may be times when you come across someone who lacks empathy or is unwilling to understand your perspective or needs. In such situations, effective communication becomes difficult or even impossible. It might be better to avoid such individuals altogether or explore alternative ways to approach them.

66
THE STORKS AND THE SPARROWS
Vardan Aygektsi

The sparrows begged the stork to allow them to build their nests, for safety, under his nest. And the snakes, settling in the reeds from which the stork made his nest, began to steal young chicks. It is known that the stork has a habit of turning his head, clicking over his back with his beak. The chicks thought, "He pitied us," and said, "We thank you very much: if you can't help, then at least you sympathize with us."

Original Moral
This fable means that some kings or princes cannot help their people and protect them from enemies, but they still collect taxes from the poor, and themselves give in to debauchery.

Modern Insight
Although sympathy and support are often appreciated, they may not always be sufficient to address a problem. In such cases, taking action becomes necessary. But determining the right course of action can also be a difficult task. Thus, it is crucial to take the time to carefully evaluate the situation and plan the most effective steps to make a meaningful impact.

45/48

67
THE BEAVER
Mkhitar Gosh

The beaver was criticized by others, "Why do you often hide in the water?" And he replied, "Because they are not satisfied with taking my glands during my life, but also strip my skin after death."

Modern Insight
This fable is directed at evil lords, for they torment both in life and death.

68
THE SUN
Mkhitar Gosh

Once the sun thought of itself as a god, during its ascension. But when it descended and hid behind the earth, it came to understand its true nature.

Original Moral
The moral about kings who were proud of their victories and fame, but in the hour of death realized their futility.

69
THE FOX AND THE CRAWFISH
Vardan Aygektsi

The fox and the crawfish became friends and sowed, reaped, threshed and collected the grain in a pile. The fox said, "Let's climb that hill, and whoever gets to the pile first, let them take the wheat." They climbed the hill, and the crawfish said, "Please, as you are getting ready to run, hit me with your tail so I know when to run after you." The crawfish opened its claws, and when the fox hit its tail and ran, it clung to her tail. The fox reached the stack of the grain, looked back to see where the crawfish was, but it had already fallen on the pile and said, "In the name of God, here are three and a half measures for me." The fox was surprised, "Oh, you sneaky one, when did you come here?"

Modern Insight
Don't underestimate the power of careful planning and strategy, even if you seem small or weak. With intelligence and foresight, you can overcome even the toughest challenges. Remember that even the smallest can outsmart their opponents. Use your ingenuity to achieve your goals and never give up.

70
THE BUTTERFLIES
Mkhitar Gosh

Butterflies, while they flutter in the air, do not bring any harm, but, descending to the ground, give birth to caterpillars, destroyers of the country.

Original Moral
The fable teaches that while our consciousness (thinking) soars in the heavens, it wins and causes no harm, but when it inclines towards the earth, it generates vile thoughts and corrupts the body.

71
THE ROOSTER AND LAZY PEOPLE
Mkhitar Gosh

The rooster crowed many times and said, "God knows that for the diligent to wake up one or two cries is enough. But I call many times for the lazy. Even then, they don't wake up. I cry only to deprive them of excuses."

Original Moral
Those who are capable of understanding only need to be taught the scriptures once or twice, while repeated teachings are intended for the stubborn.

72
THE COWS
Mkhitar Gosh

Once, the cows gathered and said, "We work hard for our children and gather milk in the udder, but people take what we have earned by squeezing the nipples. Let's leave and never come back to them!" But one of them, wise, said, "This is not true, because people take only what is more than our youngsters' needs, and they care for us and our heir, and we receive more than we give." And understanding this, they became happy.

Original Moral
The fable teaches servants who think they give more than they receive from their masters, but after the instruction of the wise, realize that what they were given is less.

73
THE CRAYFISH AND ITS YOUNG
Vardan Aygektsi

The story goes that the crayfish taught its young to walk straight, while it walked crookedly. They, seeing how the mother walked, walked the same way. And when the mother threatened to punish them for walking straight, they would say, "You walk that way, and we will too!"

Original Moral
And so it is with leaders who walk crookedly and preach to the people to walk straight, but the people see how the leader walks and also walk that way.

Modern Insight
The apple doesn't fall far from the tree.

*It's time to pause! What are your thoughts?
Your pen will help connect the dots.*

74
AN OBSTINATE HORSE
Mkhitar Gosh

A horse refused to obey its rider and galloped away. As it wandered, it met a lion and ran away from it, then it met a bear and ran away from that too, and finally, it came across a wolf and other similar dangers. In the end, it returned to its owner, submitting not for the sake of food, but to escape certain death.

Modern Insight
The best lessons are often learned through direct experience.

75
GENEROSITY
Vardan Aygektsi

The story goes that someone came to King Alexander, who was very generous and asked him for a favor, and Alexander gave him a beautiful city. And the princes asked him, "Why did you give it to him? This man is not worthy of such a city." The king said, "Even though he is not worthy, I have to give him beautiful things because I am generous."

Modern Insight
To truly embody generosity, it's important to give without expecting anything in return. Follow your heart and give freely if it feels right.

76
THE FISH AND THE KING
Mkhitar Gosh

The fish were accused by their king, "Why do you eat other, smaller fish?" And they boldly said, "Because we learned from you. You consumed those who came to worship you, turning them into food." As a result, they became even bolder.

Modern Insight
As a leader you have a responsibility to set a positive example. Always be mindful of your actions, as they will have a significant impact on those around you.

77
THE POOR MAN AND THE WOLF
Vardan Aygektsi

Once a man lost his donkey and wandered around very upset, looking for it. The wolf, seeing this, asked him, "What are you looking for?" The man said, "I lost my donkey and can't find it." The wolf said, "I found your donkey." The man said, "Bring it to me, and I will give you what is appropriate for the find." The wolf said, "Your donkey was caught in the mud, and I had to struggle with it for three days before I could get it out. As a reward for finding the donkey, I ate it. I knew you were poor and couldn't reward me any other way."

Modern Insight
Not everyone who appears helpful has good intentions, and some people may use deceit to appear virtuous.

78
THE JUJUBE TREE[18] AND THE FOOL
Mkhitar Gosh

Once a fool cut down a jujube tree, mistaking it for a Jerusalem thorn. The angered tree said, "O merciless one, a plant should be recognized by its fruits, not by its appearance."

Modern Insight
Rushing into something without proper knowledge or consideration can lead to costly mistakes and regrets. Instead, take the time to assess the situation and weigh the consequences of your actions.

---

[18] The jujube tree (*Ziziphus vulgaris*) bears fruits and is covered with thorns.

79
THE DONKEY AT THE WEDDING
Vardan Aygektsi

The donkey was honored and invited to the wedding of the king's son. And the donkey said, "I am not a musician or a dancing master, and therefore I am in trouble. I fear that they either have prepared a heavy load for me, or I will have to carry water for the wedding."

Original Moral
Tell this fable when you are called to a task or activity that is inappropriate, mismatched or beyond your capabilities.

80
THE BLACKSMITH AND THE CARPENTER
Mkhitar Gosh

When King Alexander was building a palace, he glorified the blacksmith more than the carpenter. And the carpenter and the farmer envied the blacksmith. One said that he creates housing and the other - food. The king heard about this and, being a wise man himself, called on other wise men to decide who to give honors. And they replied, "It is said that Adam first cultivated the earth, but blacksmithing was established earlier, as the blacksmith made tools for himself, for the carpenter, and the farmer. Therefore, the blacksmith is first to honor, and the farmer needs both." And they convinced the carpenter and the farmer not to envy.

Modern Insight
Envy shoots at others and wounds itself.

81
THE BLACKSMITH AND THE COPPERSMITH[19]
Mkhitar Gosh

The coppersmith and the blacksmith, having become friends, once began to boast about their crafts; they even went to court before the elders. And they recognized the blacksmith as more respectable, saying, "Useful for everyone-worthy of honor."

Original Moral
*This fable shows that there is nothing
more worthy of honor than usefulness for all,
in both physical and spiritual matters.*

---

[19] A coppersmith, also known as a brazier, is a person who makes artifacts from copper and brass.

82
A FLEA AND A PRINCE
Vardan Aygektsi

A prince was greatly troubled by a flea and cleverly caught her. The flea said, "I beg you, do not kill me, for the harm I have caused you is so small." But the prince said, "All that is within your power, you have done!"

Original Moral
The fable shows that it is proper for princes, kings, and judges to pursue even the minor criminal so that the major criminals are intimidated.

83
A MAN AND A WATERMELON
Mkhitar Gosh

A man entered a garden and wanted to cut and eat a watermelon. The watermelon, in horror, said, "What are you doing? Don't you know that I am an egg dropped by an elephant? If you take me to your home, take care of me, and ensure I don't crack, I will give birth to a baby elephant worth a thousand dahekans." And the man, delighted, obeyed and took care of it, and when it had completely rotted, he threw it away. In this way, the watermelon avoided the knife.

Original Moral
This fable wants to convey to us the thought that if we happen to fall into the hands of a murderer, we should pretend to be someone who is highly respected and well-regarded, in the hopes that they will take us to their home for a ransom and we can avoid the sword either by becoming ill or passing away.

84
THE FISH OR THE CAT
Vardan Aygektsi

A man bought a fish that weighed one liter[20] and brought it home, then left. His wife cooked it and served it to her friend. In the evening, when the man returned home, he said, "Give me the fish, I want to eat." The wife replied, "The cat ate it." So, the man took the cat, weighed it, and it weighed exactly one liter. He said, "If this is the cat, then where is the fish? And if this is the fish, then where is the cat?"

Modern Insight
Asking proper questions can reveal falsehoods and expose liars. Be thoughtful and strategic in the questions you ask, especially when you suspect someone is not telling the truth.

---

[20] A "litra" or "liter" was a unit of weight measurement in medieval Armenia, approximately equal to 325 grams.

85
THE BANDIT AND THE PRIEST
Mkhitar Gosh

A bandit once grabbed a priest and wanted to kill him. But then a spirit of strength came upon the priest and he overpowered the bandit and beat him as he deserved. And the bandit begged for mercy, saying, "You are a priest and always repeat: peace to all and other similar things." The priest said, "Oh, evil-doer, I am beating you for the sake of preserving peace for all because you do not love peace."

86
THE FOX AND THE PARTRIDGE
Vardan Aygektsi

The fox, catching a partridge, held it in her jaws and wanted to eat it. And the partridge said, "Blessed be the God who has called me to his kingdom, for I am leaving these earthly evils; you, fox, praise God and then eat me, and great good will come to you." The fox sat down, opened her jaws, looked at the sky, and said, "I praise you, O good God, who has provided me with a good meal." The partridge slipped out of the fox's jaws and flew away. And the fox said, "Oh, I am crazy and foolish! I should have tasted it first, and then praised God."

Original Moral
This fable shows: do not consider what is promised as yours and do not thank anyone until you receive it. If you are given water, then immediately drink it, for many promise but fail to follow through, revealing their true nature as liars.

87
THE BABY CAMEL, THE FOAL[21] AND THE PIGS
Vardan Aygektsi

The baby camel and the foal cried and told their parents, "We are miserable and hungry, jealousy is eating us up. The piglets are given a lot of barley, but we have been driven away." And their parents said, "Bear with it; the time will come when you will pity them." Winter came, and the pigs were being slaughtered. The foal and the baby camel heard the terrible squeal; they shuddered and asked their parents, "Why are they squealing?" The parents led them and showed them the slaughtered pigs, and they lifted their hooves and said, "Oh, look, has even a single barley grain stuck to our feet? If it has, pick it up."

Modern Insight
Be content with what you have and don't envy others. Generally, things are not what they seem on the surface, and you never know what challenges or struggles others may be facing. Instead of focusing on what others have, appreciate what's yours and be grateful for it.

---

[21] A foal is a young donkey or horse that is less than one year old.

88
THE MULE
Mkhitar Gosh

A mule was reproached that he is the son of a donkey, but he boasted of his mother, a horse. But he lost the argument because the father's lineage is more important than the mother's.

Original Moral
The meaning of the fable is clear,
for rule and everything else should be according to the father's lineage and not the mother's.

89
THE MOON
Mkhitar Gosh

At full moon, the moon imagined it was the sun and could shine during the day. But when it was waning, it did not shine at night either.

Original Moral
The story condemns those who, when they attain a position of respect in something, think they have reached the status of the greats, and, in their madness, lose even what they have.

90
THE BRAVE WARRIOR
Vardan Aygektsi

A wise warrior, lame in both legs, was going to war, and someone from the warriors asked him, "Oh unfortunate, worthy of crying, where are you going? They will kill you now since you can't run away!" And he said, "Brother, in times of war, one must not flee, but to stand one's ground, fight and emerge victorious."

Modern Insight
The advice people give is often a reflection of their beliefs and actions. Pay attention to the advice people give to others, and you can gain insight into their character and values.

91
THE PHILOSOPHER AT THE FEAST
Vardan Aygektsi

A philosopher was invited to dine at the royal table. He sat with the guests, and a wine bearer brought him a golden cup of wine. He stood up and said, "Good king, I drink this wine to your glory." And he poured the wine onto the ground. The barons laughed and said, "You are crazy, philosopher!" And he replied, "You are worthy of laughter, because here the wine has been spilled on the ground, but if I had drunk it, it would have spilled me on the ground."

Modern Insight
Stand by your own beliefs and values, even if it goes against the popular opinion. Don't blindly follow others, even if they are in a position of authority. Evaluate every piece of advice carefully, and choose what's right for you.

92
THE OLD WARRIOR
Mkhitar Gosh

A certain brave warrior received an order from the king to fight as a knight in battle against a single combatant from another king. Being scared of his old age, he came up with the idea of dyeing his hair and beard. But it didn't help him in the battle, and he was defeated.

Modern Insight
Always stay true to yourself, as pretending to be someone you're not can often lead to failure and disappointment. Instead, accept yourself for who you are and work towards improving your skills and abilities.

93
THE WILD BOAR AND THE FOX
Vardan Aygektsi

A wild boar was carefully sharpening its tusks. A fox came by and said, "What are you trying to do? There's no danger of war or battles right now." The wild boar replied, "Be quiet, you worthless fox; you know nothing about war. If I wait for it to sharpen my weapons, it will be too late."

Modern Insight
Consistent practice is essential to mastery in any profession. Those who are truly dedicated to their craft will continue to practice even when there is no immediate need, knowing that preparation is key to ongoing success.

94
THE CAT AND THE MICE
Mkhitar Gosh

The mice sent a messenger to the cat and said, "What have we done to you that you are chasing us? We don't eat anything of yours." And he replied, "Don't you know that people feed us to guard their barns? If you don't go there, feel free to move around, I won't harm you." And, putting his paw to his head, he confirmed this with an oath. The mice, emboldened, wanted to pick up the fallen grains, but the cat sprang and caught many of them. They said, "Are you not sworn not to seek revenge from us for the fallen grains?" And he said, "I did not swear, I just touched my paw to my head out of habit."

Modern Insight
Beware of those who deceive with false promises and friendly faces. Recognize their true intentions and protect yourself by avoiding them.

95
THE OLD DONKEY
Vardan Aygektsi

Donkeys were walking in a herd on a royal business. Among them was one, the oldest, seasoned by years and plumper than others, and they all highly respected him. They were climbing a mountain, and the old donkey loudly roared and let out a terrible thunder from behind. The other donkeys approached and said, "Oh, venerable father, your front voice was usual for us, but what was that terrible noise that came from the other end? Please tell us!" He replied, "My children, I will not lie to you, and I will tell you the truth: because of the strength of my front voice, I do not know what other noise and thunder may happen on my other side."

96
THE RAM
Mkhitar Gosh

The ram repeatedly struck his horns against the tree and broke them, and began to curse and blame the tree. And the tree replied, "You are to blame yourself, why do you blame me?"

Original Moral
This fable censures those who foolishly lash out with curses, who, in a fit of rage over their faults, blame others.

97
THE TURTLE AND THE HORSE
Olympian

The turtle challenged the horse to a race. When the appointed day came, the horse indulged in pleasure and idleness, while the turtle engaged in training, constant exercises, and developing agility. When it was time for the competition and the seats were filled with spectators, the horse and turtle, facing each other, stood at the starting line and received the signal to start running. The horse, having been idle for so long, was stiff and couldn't even take a step, while the turtle completed the race faster than anyone expected and emerged triumphant.

Original Moral
Don't rely solely on nature:
you also need to apply the necessary efforts
and strive in everything.

98
THE SHEEP AND THE GOATS
Mkhitar Gosh

Sheep, walking in the herd, shook their fat tails[22]. The goats began criticizing them, "Why don't you walk modestly, like us?" But they were blaming the sheep more out of envy than modesty.

Original Moral
This fable aims against the habit of envious people: if someone succeeds due to their qualities, they are criticized, while they consider themselves modest because they lack those qualities.

---

[22] In Armenian culture, sheep with fat tails are highly valued for their meat and wool.

99
THE PEACOCK AND THE PIGEON
Vardan Aygektsi

The birds gathered, picked a peacock for its beauty, and anointed him king. The pigeon came and said, "Good king, if eagles come to oppress us, what help can you give us?"

Original Moral
This fable demonstrates that it befits a king not only to be beautiful, but also to be brave, to have military strength, and to have versatile wisdom in all aspects.

100
THE CABBAGE
Mkhitar Gosh

The cabbage praised itself as a cure for the stomach, "If you eat me in raw form, I will weaken, and in cooked form I will strengthen." And he lied about many other things. Someone, believing, began to eat cabbage, expecting benefits and instead began to hear noises from his stomach. He cursed the cabbage as a liar and cheat, but she responded, "Since I was able to penetrate your stomach, what do I care if I come out with curses?"

Original Moral
This fable is aimed at those who lie and cheat in order to gain fame. When exposed and scorned, they are not upset because the deception has succeeded.

101
THE PEACOCK AND EAGLE
Mkhitar Gosh

The peacock, showing off all its beauty, was praised and he began to think of seizing the throne. Some wise birds advised him not to listen to the words of temptation and that the reign is by birthright. But he did not listen to them. The king of birds heard about this and, appearing, defeated and killed the peacock's children and his entire family. Many plucked his wings and feathers, leaving him barenaked. He did not achieve the reign and lost his beauty.

Original Moral
Many, tempted by the words of instigators, were deceived by the hope of ruling based on only one's luck, but, ultimately failing to achieve their goal, lost even what they had.

102
THE DEATH OF THE EAGLE
Vardan Aygektsi

As the eagle soared through the sky, an arrow struck him. Bewildered, he looked back, and saw the arrow with his own feather, and said, "Woe is me, for behold, from me is the cause of my death."

103
LEVIATHAN
Mkhitar Gosh

After the princes were appointed over the waters, they said, "Oh, king Leviathan! Why do you not make circumnavigations of your possessions and make raids?" And he said, "Because we have no enemies and we have no need for anything. Let us enjoy what is ours and we will not turn to you so as not to be a burden." And his words pleased them. If a kingdom does not suffer injury from another king and has enough for life, then it is good to be peaceful and not burden one's own with circumnavigations. But if enemies force the issue, it is not humiliating not to wage war.

Modern Insight
When there is no conflict or threat, it is perfectly fine to sit back and enjoy the moment. But if a threat arises, be prepared to defend yourself and take necessary actions to protect what is yours.

104
THE DECEIVED LION
Mkhitar Gosh

The animals came to the lion and said, "You act like a ruler in everything, but in one thing - like a coward: you cover your tracks." Afraid of sudden attacks, they wanted to remove the threat. Confused by these words, the lion began to wander without hiding, and, now knowing of his approach, they were able to escape danger, while he lost his prey.

Original Moral
This fable teaches how to get rid of evil by using both praise and criticism.

Modern Insight
Sometimes it is better to use strategy and cunning, even if it means appearing cowardly, than to act recklessly and lose opportunities.

105
TANNER AND FURRIER
Mkhitar Gosh

The tanner was passing by the door of the furrier[23], and the latter started laughing and called him smelly. As he left, the tanner cursed, saying, "If someone who was a master of golden crafts or the like had scolded me, it would have been appropriate, but how dare you, who is even more foul-smelling?"

Original Moral
This fable teaches about the many people who can't bear to be criticized by those worse than themselves, but allow the righteous to condemn them.

---

[23] A furrier is a person who works as a fur mechanic or leather worker, making and repairing fur and leather items. The furrier's insult was likely based on the natural odors associated with their respective trades.

106
THE FOX AND THE CAMEL
Vardan Aygektsi

The fox and the camel became friends. They came together to the river, started to cross it, and the camel went in first. The fox said, "Brother, is the river very deep?" The camel responded, "Barely knee deep." And the fox said, "Oh no, for it's one thing for a camel's knee, and another for a fox's knee."

Modern Insight
What's good for the goose is not always good for the gander.

107
ALMOND AND CHESTNUT
Mkhitar Gosh

Almond trees, bitter and sweet, are brothers from the same mother but different fathers. The sweet almond, suffering from the bitterness of his brother, made the sweet chestnut his friend and brother, finding him to his liking because of the similar qualities. When many criticized him, he said, "He who is chosen by my will, that is my brother." And no one could argue with him.

Original Moral
This fable is clear. Even if people are born as siblings they turn out to be incompatible with each other in character. They will separate as necessary and prefer strangers who are similar in temperament. And even though they are criticized for this, no one will be able to prove their righteousness in this criticism.

108
THE WIDOW AND THE PRINCE
Vardan Aygektsi

There was a prince, very cruel and wicked. A widow lived in the same city, and the prince, demanding taxes, oppressed her, and the widow prayed to God to protect the prince from harm. They went and told the prince, "In response to your evil, the widow prays for you!" The prince came and said, "I have not done you any good, why are you praying for me!" She said, "Your father was a bad man, I cursed him, and he died; you sat in his place, and you are even worse than him; I fear that if you die, your son will be even worse than you."

Modern Insight
The grass isn't always greener on the other side. What may seem bad now may actually be a blessing in disguise, as things could always be worse.

109
THE MAGPIE
Mkhitar Gosh

Usually, the magpie in the forest constantly cries, especially if it sees any of the animals. When the chick asked her about the reason, she replied, "So that my enemies always see me alert and don't think of hunting."

Modern Insight
An ounce of prevention is worth a pound of cure.

110
SWALLOW'S NEST
Mkhitar Gosh

The swallow, trying to escape from hunters, made a nest for herself under the beams of the roof. And, feeling cramped from domestic enemies, mice, she took a hair from a cat and put it in the nest, and her chicks remained unharmed.

Original Moral
This fable teaches us through the wisdom of this bird: when settled in a fortress, we protect ourselves from external enemies and experience oppression from domestic enemies, we find help against them in the same household.

111
A BEGGAR'S PRAYER
Vardan Aygektsi

A poor man was on his way to a certain city. He fell ill on the road and prayed to God to send a mount to take him to a place to stay. And then someone ill-tempered came riding up, beat him, and said, "Get up, put my foal on your back, as it can't keep up with its mother." The beggar got up and cried bitterly, as he could barely stand, and the other one kept beating him. And the beggar said, "Woe is me, Oh God! Instead of relieving me, you have made my suffering worse."

Original Moral
This fable demonstrates that the poor suffer from poverty and ask God for wealth and prosperity, while kings and tyrants take away and rob what they have.

112
THE AXES AND THE TREES
Vardan Aygektsi

Lumberjacks took axes, went into the forest, and began to cut down trees. And the trees said, "What are they doing?" And the cypress said, "Woe to us, brothers, for the handles of that which they are cutting us with are from us."

Modern Insight
Sometimes we can unwittingly facilitate our own downfall by providing the tools to those who would harm us. Be mindful of the consequences of your actions and decisions, and try to anticipate any potential negative outcome.

113
THE PRIEST AND THE BIRDS
Mkhitar Gosh

On Easter, all the birds came and confessed and all took Communion[24]. The hawk and the crow came as well and also confessed to the priest, "We don't know of any other sin but that we hunted mice and frogs and ate them." And the priest, calling them nasty, excluded them. Leaving, they caught chicks and presented them to the priest. Tempted by this, he excused both, saying, "You didn't know how to confess before, because what you ate were old birds that had already lost their wings!" And he took Communion with them.

Original Moral
This fable hints at greedy priests. For they drive away from the church those who are committing adultery, as well as other reprobates, by frightening them, and then for a bribe, they receive them back again, making up some pretexts, and administer communion.

---

[24] Communion is a Christian sacrament or ritual in which a person receives bread and wine, which are believed to be the body and blood of Jesus Christ. It is also known as the Eucharist, the Lord's Supper, or the Holy Communion. The practice of Communion has been a central part of Christian worship since the time of Jesus, who is said to have instituted it at the Last Supper with his disciples. The act of sharing in Communion is seen as a way to connect with God, receive forgiveness for sins, and unite with other members of the church community.

114
CUCUMBER AND MELON
Mkhitar Gosh

The cucumber, ripening early, considered himself more respectable than other vegetables, but the melon scolded him, "You are in high regard as long as I am not here, but upon my arrival, you are disregarded because when you are ripe, you are tasteless."

Original Moral
This fable suggests that unworthy individuals first enjoy honor, but when worthy individuals appear, they become disregarded; and the longer it goes on, the more obvious their unworthiness becomes.

115
DONKEY THE GRANDFATHER
Vardan Aygektsi

A donkey received good news. "Rejoice, be happy, and accept gifts, because a grandson has been born to you." And the donkey said, "Alas, my friends! Even if a hundred grandsons are born from my loins, they will not ease the weight of the packsaddle on my back."

Modern Insight
You have a unique path to walk in life, with your own set of challenges and triumphs. No one else can walk your path for you. So embrace it, make the most of it, and fulfill your own destiny.

116
THE SNAIL AND THE HEDGEHOG
Mkhitar Gosh

The hedgehog tried to convince the snail, saying, "Come out so I can treat you and honor you in every way!" The snail replied, "No one sees you as hospitable towards others. So why would you be like that to me? It's not about that; it's about your thirst for my blood!" And she didn't come out, saved from him thanks to her caution.

Modern Insight
Be discerning when dealing with others to prevent costly mistakes. Before putting your trust in someone, take the time to understand who they are, what their motives are, and whether or not they have your best interests in mind. As the old proverb goes, "Fool me once, shame on you. Fool me twice, shame on me."

*You've read a lot! Hey, way to go!
Unleash your thoughts and let them flow.*

117
THE LITTLE SPARROW
Vardan Aygektsi

King Solomon fell ill. All the animals came to visit him except for the little sparrow. He said, "I am greater than Solomon." Later, he repented and came. Solomon asked, "Did you say you were better than me?" The little sparrow replied, "I knew you were wise and would understand me. What was I supposed to do? When the messengers arrived, I was sitting next to my girlfriend!"

Modern Insight
*If you're going to talk the talk,
make sure you can walk the walk.*

118
THE CAMELS AND THE FOXES
Vardan Aygektsi

Three camels and three foxes became friends and found three white loaves of bread. The camels took the bread, raised their heads, and, grumbling, chewed the bread, while the foxes cried at their feet. And the camels, stepping on them, killed them.

Modern Insight
Be careful who you befriend. Choose your friends wisely and don't trust everyone blindly.

119
THE HYENA AND THE LION
Mkhitar Gosh

The lion captured the hyena for theft, and she said, "I eat the dead because I cannot handle the living, but you, since you are powerful, constantly do this."

Original Moral
This fable condemns abusive princes, for they punish thieves while committing the same acts of violence.

120
THE BADGER AND THE FOX
Mkhitar Gosh

The fox asked the badger, "Why am I always thin, and why are you so fat?" The badger replied, "Because I don't look for much and eat everything I find."

121
THE ENCHANTED LION
Olympian

A lion, amazed by the beauty of the girl, was consumed by passion and, approaching her father, asked for her hand. But the father, terrified, was reluctant to refuse directly. He cleverly brought up excuses to the lion and said, "I would be happy to be related to you, but my daughter is afraid of your claws and huge fangs. If you drop them and come, you will become even more desired and be a beautiful groom!" The lion agreed because he was completely carried away by passion. And, tearing out his claws and fangs, he came for the girl. But upon entering he was stoned, as he was defenseless.

Original Moral
This fable teaches many not to lay down their natural weapons.

122
THE FOX AND THE HUNTERS
Vardan Aygektsi

Hunters chased foxes with dogs. One of the foxes turned around and said, "Please tell me, what is the reason you are pursuing us?" The hunters replied, "To take your skin." And she said, "Lord God, thank you that this is all they want! I thought they wanted to make me the supervisor of poultry farming in this district or the keeper of the chicken coop."

Modern Insight
Keeping your cool and a sense of humor in stressful situations is a valuable virtue to possess. Humor helps to diffuse tension and relieve stress, making it easier to think clearly and find solutions to problems.

123
THE CONFIDENT IGNORAMUS
Vardan Aygektsi

Someone was asked, "Have you seen a bathhouse?" He replied, "I even tasted its meat!" Then they asked, "What does it look like?" He said, "It has the same horn as a pig." Then they said, "Well, this person has not only never seen a bathhouse, but also never seen a pig."

Modern Insight
Honesty is your best policy. Don't pretend to know something you don't, or you risk losing credibility. The truth may be uncomfortable at first, but it's definitely respected in the long run.

124
THE POTTER'S DOG
Vardan Aygektsi

A wolf stole livestock, and the shepherds' dogs chased after him. The potter's dog was also chasing and pressing the wolf. The wolf turned around and said, "Cursed potter's dog, what am I carrying off from you, a pestle, a scraper, or a stick for polishing pots?"

Modern Insight
Sometimes, we can feel pressured to conform to popular opinions or beliefs, even if they do not align with our own values or knowledge. Blindly following the crowd can lead to loss of individuality and even mistakes. Remember, it's okay to stand out, as long as it is based on our own thoughts and beliefs. Be yourself, everyone else is already taken.

125
THE RABBITS AND THE FROGS
Vardan Aygektsi

Once, thirty rabbits gathered, consulted, and said, "Let's all go to the sea together to escape this bitter life. We were created too weak: animals or birds, they all eat us. It's better for us to die than to live such a miserable life." When they ran to the sea, they saw a multitude of frogs, and with a shout, the frogs jumped and hid in the water. And seeing that the frogs were weaker than themselves, the rabbits thanked God.

Original Moral
Oh man, don't look at those who are higher than you, but look down at those who are poorer than you and take comfort. And if you have sinned, don't look at the very righteous, but look at the many sinners and take comfort.

126
THE COMBATIVE BULL
Mkhitar Gosh

The bull wanted to butt his owner, but he couldn't and grumbled at God, "He made my horns not straight, but curved." And the owner, answering him, said, "God knew your wicked nature, that's why he thought up to grow your horns this way."

Original Moral
This fable applies to the vengeful, for God never allows them to exact revenge as they desire.

127
THE OSTRICH AND THE SPARROW
Mkhitar Gosh

The sparrow, seeing the ostrich carrying big eggs, was tempted and asked for the secret. The ostrich said, "I eat fire, and that's why I carry big eggs." Thinking that what he said was true, the sparrow ate fire and died. He didn't think that the reason was not in that at all, but in his height.

Original Moral
The fable accuses superficial desires that the small, seeing the work of the strong, want to act on their own without thinking about their own weakness.

128
GOLD AND WHEAT
Mkhitar Gosh

Gold declared itself the ruler and demanded that all other matter bow to it as king. All came and bowed except for wheat, which said, "I will wait until it bows to me first."

Original Moral
*This fable shows that the position of things is changeable,
for they are not always honored; sometimes
one or another is magnified, and sometimes it is stripped of honor.
But, due to the frequent danger of hunger,
all matter bends before the power of wheat.*

129
THE FOX AND THE DOGS
Vardan Aygektsi

The fox was asked, "How many different tricks do you know?" And the fox said, "A hundred different tricks I use against the dog. But my best trick is not to let the dog or myself see each other."

Modern Insight
The best victory is the one that doesn't require fighting. Avoiding conflicts and finding peaceful solutions can prevent unnecessary harm and ensure a safe outcome for everyone involved. As the Japanese martial arts saying goes, "The ultimate aim of martial arts is not having to use them."

130
THE MARTEN[25] AND THE MOUSE
Olympian

A marten was consumed with passion for a young man and begged the goddess Astghik[26] to allow her to become a beautiful woman. Once her wish was granted, she became a beautiful woman by appearance. But after a wedding celebration with her beloved, with songs and dances and the lights burning brightly at the bridal bed, she, seeing a mouse running by, chased after it to catch it.

Modern Insight
Recognize and work on your bad habits in order to better yourself. Cultivating good habits takes time and effort, but it's worth it for your own well-being and happiness.

---

[25] The marten is a type of mammal in the weasel family. It has a long, slender body and a bushy tail. It is found in boreal and temperate forests of the Northern Hemisphere, including North America and Eurasia.

[26] Astghik was a goddess worshiped in Armenian mythology as the patroness of love, beauty, and fertility. She was often depicted with flowers, especially roses, and was associated with the planet Venus. In Armenian folklore, she was regarded as the protector of young women and children, and was invoked for blessings of fertility and happiness in love.

131
THE WOLF AND THE FOX
Vardan Aygektsi

The wolf chased a herd of deer and ran after one of them until it was exhausted. He cornered the deer in a ravine to tear it apart. Suddenly, a fox came out of its den, jumped into the water, shook itself off, and ran to the wolf panting, "Uncle, here we are, and we've caught it." The wolf replied, "Oh, you rapscallion, where were you when I was chasing the deer from ravine to ravine?" The fox said, "The excitement made you blind, and you didn't see me. I was running from ravine to ravine as well, and I am sweating all over."

Modern Insight
Success is like a magnet for fake friends. Be wary of those who only come around when the gravy train has arrived. They're like flies on a cake, they're only interested in the sweet stuff and couldn't care less about the flour and eggs that went into making it. Stick with the true friends who were always by your side, through your ups and downs.

132
THE PANTHER
Mkhitar Gosh

After chasing prey and losing it, the panther beat and cursed her cub in anger, then, repenting, regretted it.

Original Moral
This fable criticizes the cruel-hearted people who, if something bad happens, impatiently distress their household, and then regret it.

133
THE BIRD AND THE HORSE
Mkhitar Gosh

An Indian king had a bird that laid eggs of pearls and precious stones. A Greek king heard of this and desired to have it. He sent ambassadors and asked for the bird. The Indian king gave it, but asked for his horse in return, which was faster than birds. Although the mutual requests were heavy, both kings immediately fulfilled them. But the bird, upon arriving to Greece, began to lay eggs like other birds, and the horse, reaching India, started to limp and did not run anymore. The Indian king returned the horse with sharp rebukes. The bird was also sent back with annoyance. And the horse and bird, returning to their place, became the same as before.

Original Moral
This fable means nothing else but that the wealth of each kingdom is given by God, and although the kings try to transfer them to each other, they cannot.

134
THE LIZARDS AND THE MOLE
Mkhitar Gosh

The king of animals ordered all his subjects to gather before him, and they all came without delay. Even the agama, the lizards and the mole came to receive gifts (for the king summoned the animals to honor each one according to their rank), and everyone laughed at them. The lion rewarded everyone and addressed them too, "What service will you carry out to receive gifts from me?" The agama and the lizard said, "We know how to crawl through stones, penetrate the locks of your enemies, our ruler. If we cannot win, we will lead the army there." The mole said, "We penetrate cities, and cut off water springs." Pleased with their answers, the lion honored even them; the ones who were greatly despised by many.

Original Moral
This fable demonstrates that all people, great and small, are needed, not only by kings, but by all princes and commoners, as well as in churches.

Modern Insight
It is important to recognize the value and importance of every profession, no matter how small or seemingly unimportant it may seem. Every job has its purpose and contributes to the functioning of society as a whole. Do not judge or look down on someone's profession based on societal expectations or stereotypes. Every person and their job deserves respect and recognition for the role they play in making our world work.

135
THE WOLF, THE GAZELLE, AND THE LION
Mkhitar Gosh

The wolf waited for the gazelle to fall asleep so he could catch her. Realizing his intention, the gazelle did not sleep for many days, while the wolf eventually fell asleep from exhaustion. Then the lion came and killed the wolf.

Modern Insight
Be vigilant, patient and careful and you can avoid danger and harm. Help can arrive from unexpected sources.

136
THE NAIVE THIEVES
Vardan Aygektsi

Two men with ill intent climbed atop a wealthy house, eager to steal the riches within. The moon shone bright and the homeowner became aware of the thieves' presence. His wife asked, "Where did you obtain all these treasures and gold, my love?" The man replied, "I used to climb down from wealthy homes in the light of the moon, just like now. I would embrace the moonbeam and speak a magical phrase, causing all the silks within the house to appear before me. I'd then tie them to the beam and ascend with my spoils." The thieves, entranced by the man's tale, foolishly hugged the moonbeams, tumbling down from the roof and meeting their unfortunate end.

Modern Insight
Beware the blinding allure of greed and do not covet what belongs to others. For the consequences of such actions may bring about one's downfall.

137
THE WILL ABOUT THE TREASURE
Vardan Aygektsi

A wise and poor man had lazy sons. At the time of his death, he called them and said, "Oh, children, my ancestors buried many treasures in our garden, and I will not show you the place. The one who works hard and digs deeply will find them." After the father's death, the sons started digging the ground with great diligence because each wanted to find the treasure himself. And the garden began to grow and thrive, and gave abundant harvests, and enriched them with treasures.

Modern Insight
The fable teaches us that hard work and diligence can lead to success and wealth. Moreover, when you love what you do and work hard, the rewards can be even more fulfilling, bringing both joy and professional growth.

138
THE REED AND THE TREES
Vardan Aygektsi

The king went for a walk in the mountains and valleys. And he saw that there were big trees broken and destroyed, and only one reed was standing, whole and intact. And the king said, "Oh, reed, tell me how you remained steadfast when such big trees were destroyed." And the reed said, "Oh, king, when the strong wind rose, the trees proudly stood against the wind, and the wind broke them, but I bent to the will of the wind and here I stand."

Modern Insight
Those who appear weaker can actually prove to be stronger than the rigid because of their flexibility and adaptability to the circumstances.

139
THE FOX AND THE NOTE-BEARING WOLF
Vardan Aygektsi

The fox found a written note, gave it to the wolf and said, "I've worked hard, and through good intermediaries, I got permission from the prince for you. Every village you encounter on your way will give you a sheep." And so she deceived the wolf, and they went together to the village, and the fox sat on a hill and gave the note to the wolf. When the wolf entered the village, the dogs and people chased and mauled him. The wounded wolf barely escaped and reached the fox. And the fox said, "Why didn't you show the note I gave you?" And the wolf replied, "I did show it, but there were a thousand dogs in the village who couldn't read."

Original Moral
The fable shows that you should not argue with the ignorant, but use wisdom and flee from demons and their servants.

140
THE LION AND THE MAN
Vardan Aygektsi

On the road sat a powerful lion, and all kinds of beasts passed tremblingly along that road. And the lion asked them, "Why are you so scared, and from whom are you running in horror?" And they said, "Run you too, because a man is coming." And the lion asked, "Who is this man and what is he, and what is his strength, and what does he look like that you are running from him?" And they said, "He will come, see you, and you will regret it." And here came a simple peasant from his field. And the lion said, "Are you the man that the beasts are running from?" And he said, "Yes, it's me." The lion said, "Let's fight." The man said, "Yes, but your weapon is with you, and mine is at home. Allow me to tie you up first so you don't run away. I'll go and get my weapon, and then we'll fight." The lion said, "Swear that you'll come back, and I'll listen to you." The man swore, and the lion said, "Now tie me up and go, and come back quickly." The man took out a rope, tied the lion tightly to an oak tree, cut a branch from the tree and began to beat the lion. And the lion exclaimed, "If you're a man, beat me harder and mercilessly on the ribs, because that befits my mind."

Original Moral
The parable shows that many strong people, being deceived by weaker ones, reproach and punish themselves like this lion.

141
A MAN AND THE WOLF
Vardan Aygektsi

A man caught a wolf, tied his legs, and, putting it on his donkey, carried it home. People, seeing him, asked, "What are you carrying on your donkey?" "I am bringing home," said the man, "to have him milked, and my children would be fed a little." "Fool," the people said, "he has ripped milking cows from all over the world, and you are taking him to milk instead?"

Modern Insight
We all have bad habits that we cling to, even though we know deep down that they are harmful or counterproductive. It's easy to get caught up in our routines and lose sight of the damage that they may cause. To avoid regret and harm down the line, we must be willing to acknowledge and let go of our bad habits, even if it takes effort and discipline.

142
THE CORRUPTED JUDGE AND THE JUG OF BUTTER
Vardan Aygektsi

A man went to the city judge and promised, "I will give you a jug of butter if tomorrow when I come to court with my opponent, you acquit me." And the next day, when they arrived in court, the judge acquitted him and, having written the verdict, gave it to him. The one who promised the butter filled the jug with straw to the edges, put two or three ladles of butter on top, corked the jug's neck, and took it to the judge. A few days later, the judge told his servant, "I want rice with butter, bring the one that the man brought and cook the rice." The servant lit a fire, put a skillet on it, brought the jug of butter, opened it, and as soon as he stuck a spoon in it, the straw came out full. The judge, realizing that he was cheated, said, "All right, I'll take care of it." One day, this man was passing by the judge's door. Seeing him, the judge called him and said, "Oh man, in your verdict that I gave you that day, I wrote one thing less. You are a poor man, bring it, I will write it down so that your opponent will not drag you to court again." "Judge," said the man, "If anything is missing at all, it's missing from the jug I gave you, but I am happy with my verdict."

Modern Insight
If you try to cheat, you might end up eating straw. Corruption might get you ahead for a moment, but in the end, it will only lead to your downfall. Plus, it's always better to have a clean conscience and a clear verdict than a jug full of lies.

143
A MAN, A NUT AND A WATERMELON
Vardan Aygektsi

A man planted a watermelon under a walnut tree. And during the harvest, he came and saw large watermelons and looking up at the tree, he saw that the nuts were small. Then he said, "Good Lord, everything you have created is perfect, except for these two fruits. They are chaotic and don't look like anything else." The man wanted to say that watermelons should be on the tree instead of walnuts, and walnuts should be on the watermelon bush. And he lay under the tree and looked at it. Suddenly, a nut fell from the tree, hit him hard on the forehead and split his forehead so that blood began to flow. And the man stood up and screamed, "Good Lord, everything you have created is in order and perfect! Whoever doesn't like what you created, may their forehead be worse than mine, because if instead of a walnut, there was a watermelon, I would be dead."

Modern Insight

The fable teaches us a valuable lesson: we are not superior to the natural world around us. Everything in the universe has been created in perfect order and harmony. Despite our technological advancements and achievements, we are still at the mercy of the forces of nature. We must learn to respect and appreciate the intricate balance of the natural world, instead of trying to impose our own will upon it. Our planet is our host, and we are its guests. Let's remember that, because by accepting and respecting its order, we can live in harmony with it.

144
RICH IN-LAW AND THE MAIDEN
Vardan Aygektsi

A wealthy man went to ask for a girl for his son according to a traditional custom. The maiden, who was being asked for, came, sat beside him, and said, "Father, your arrival is blessed. It would be good if, when you come next time, we went to Rome, from there to Jerusalem and then to the Khor Virap[32]." "My daughter," said the man, "I came to take you home. Do you want to deprive me of my home[33]?"

Modern Insight

Be mindful of the impact of our desires on others, especially people we don't know. While it is important to have dreams and aspirations, we should also consider the practicalities and consequences of our actions on those around us. Try to find a balance between pursuing our own goals and being considerate of others.

---

[32] Khor Virap is an Armenian Orthodox monastery located in the Ararat plain in Armenia, near the border with Turkey. It is one of the most important pilgrimage sites in the country and is believed to be the location where St. Gregory the Illuminator was imprisoned for 13 years before converting King Tiridates III to Christianity, making Armenia the first country to adopt Christianity as its state religion in the early 4th century.

[33] The man is expressing concern that the cost of the suggested travels to Rome, Jerusalem, and Khor Virap would be so high that it could jeopardize his financial stability and ability to maintain his homestead.

145
THE FOX AND THE GEESE
Vardan Aygektsi

A fox entered the goose's nest. And their nature is such that they began to hiss, saying, "Ssssss[34]!" "Oh, if you'll be quiet," said the fox, "I will be all the more."

---

[34] In the original language, the geese say "Souuusss" or "Սուս" in Armenian, which translates to "be quiet."

146
THE HAWK AND THE DOMESTIC CHICKEN
Vardan Aygektsi

The hawk accused the chicken and said to him, "Why are you so ungrateful to your master? Why do you fear him? Don't you see that I, despite being a wild bird, as soon as my master whistles or calls out with a wave of his hand, I immediately come to him? And you, even though you were born and raised with your family in his house, you avoid him." The chicken replied, "I remember the spit-roaster because many of us were grilled, but none of the falcons. O king of birds, if you had seen one hawk on a spit-roaster, I think you too would turn away from man, and even if you were convinced and being promised many rewards a thousand times, you would not agree to obey his call again."

Modern Insight
When you find yourself criticizing and accusing others, remember that you may not always have the full picture. Take the time to listen to others and develop empathy to gain a better understanding of their perspective and avoid making hasty judgments.

147
THE HONOR OF ROBES
Vardan Aygektsi

The king was traveling with his army and saw two holy fathers in unattractive clothes. The king got off his horse, bowed, and kissed them. His princes began to complain that the king honored the small people instead of showing respect to those of great stature. When the king learned about this, he ordered to make four chests: two externally beautiful, but full of garbage and sand, and two other externally unpleasant, rough, full of gold and jewelry inside. And calling the slandering princes, the king said, "Evaluate and choose which of the four sealed boxes you want." They chose the beautiful ones, and when they opened them, they saw only garbage and sand, and they regretted this. The king said, "This is how you look at the face and bright clothes of a person who is inside full of filth. And those holy fathers I encountered were poor externally, but inside they were filled with the grace of the soul."

Modern Insight
In a world that values appearance and status over inner qualities, it's easy to make assumptions about people based on their external characteristics. But what's on the surface doesn't always reflect what's on the inside. To truly know someone, we need to look beyond the external and delve deeper into their character. The inner world of each person is a complex and wondrous puzzle waiting to be discovered.

148
PRAYER OF A GREEDY MAN
Vardan Aygektsi

A greedy man who loved money more than anything else said, "My God, let everything that comes into my hands become gold and silver." And God granted his request. Everything that came into his hands immediately turned into gold and silver: bread, water, and the like. After some time, he died of hunger.

Modern Insight
When greed enters, wisdom departs.

149
THE PARABLE OF PATIENCE
Vardan Aygektsi

The teacher wanted to teach the student a virtue of patience and sent him to the cemetery to praise the tombstones. The next day he sent him to scold and berate them, and then asked, "Did the stones become proud of your praise?" He said, "No." "Did they complain about your scolding and say something?" The student replied, "Not at all." "Go ahead," said the priest, "and act in the same way. Do not be proud of praise and do not be sad about disrespect."

Modern Insight
Life is full of ups and downs, and it's important to not let either success or failure consume us. Set a time limit to celebrate or mourn, and then move on with your life. Dwelling on the past for too long will only hold you back from experiencing all the wonderful things that life has to offer. So let go of what has passed, and embrace what is yet to come.

150
ALEXANDER AND THE INDIAN ARCHER
Unknown Author

Alexander heard from an Indian archer that he could pierce a ring with an arrow. He ordered him to strike the ring. And the archer declined, for which the king became angry and ordered to kill him. And the executioner, rebuking the archer, said, "Why did you not shoot to stay alive, and now you die in vain?" And he replied, "A lot of time has passed since I took the bow in my hands. I was afraid that I would lose my fame." This was immediately reported to the king. And he was very surprised, released the man, gave many gifts for the fact that he accepted death, so that he wouldn't suddenly prove unworthy of his fame.

Modern Insight
A good reputation takes a lifetime to build, and it can be easily lost with one wrong move. Guard your name and reputation, as they are valuable assets that are hard to regain once lost.

151
THE POMEGRANATE AND THE FIG
Mkhitar Gosh

The pomegranate and the fig wanted to unite in love and pledged to be sweet, but because of the acidity of the pomegranate, fig became bored and their union broke apart.

Modern Insight
The meaning of the proverb is that lovers should first try each other's manners, are they alike in all aspects, and if not, love will easily be broken.

152
THE RASPBERRY AND THE GRAPEVINE
Mkhitar Gosh

Concealing her ill thoughts towards the grapevine, the raspberry said, "I will grow like you and bring twice as many fruits and surpass you because I don't wilt in winter." The grapevine replied, "Your bragging will be complete when you harvest in the fall." And in the fall, the raspberry was trampled.

Modern Insight
Empty vessels make the most noise. Those who boast the most often have the least to show for it. Let your actions speak for themselves, instead of relying on empty words.

153
THE PEACH AND THE QUINCE
Mkhitar Gosh

The peach criticized the quince, saying, "You look yellow and people find it hard to eat you. I look good and have a light taste." And the quince replied, "You're a liar and a deceiver of people. You seem sweet, but when you get into the stomach, you cause a lot of harm. I'm yellow because while being digested I remove the illness, and become compassionate to the sick, and not rejected by them like you."

Original Moral
The meaning of the fable is clear: liars always criticize the honest in their rough behavior and present themselves as kind and mournful. But the true words are the genuine medicine for a person, though they may seem repellent at first glance, but, empathizing with the person, they cure him from illnesses.

154
THE COTTON AND THE PLANE TREE
Mkhitar Gosh

Farmers were watering cotton fields near a plane tree[30] and telling each other to be careful not to cut down the cotton trees. Upon hearing that cotton was referred to as a tree, the plane became angry and said, "How can it be called equal to me as a tree? After all, I am so thick and tall, and occupy so much space!" And the cotton replied aloud, without hesitation, saying, "You are tall and thick, but there is no benefit from you. You are not suitable for building, you do not bear fruit, and you are not fit for firewood. Despite the large shadow, you receive more accusations than praise. While I, humble and weak, am useful not only to the rich but also to the poor. By being grown, gathered and weaved I become clothing equal to sheep's wool, flax, and silk. All you offer is acorns." Having thus scolded cotton, the plane tree fell silent.

Original Moral
My fable silences the arrogant and proud people, those who have appearance and height and live uselessly, and others who despise the weak and short, who are however suitable and useful in many things.

---

[30] A plane tree is a species of tree in the genus Platanus, also known as sycamore in some countries. It is known for its large size and distinctive, peeling bark. They are commonly used as street and park trees, and are valued for their shade and ornamental appearance.

155
THE STORK AND THE SPARROWS
Mkhitar Gosh

A flock of sparrows went to the stork and begged him, "In your nest, give us a place to raise our chicks and protect our chicks from snakes." And the stork replied, "What will you do for me in return?" And they said, "We will pray for your chicks to grow healthy, not suffering from the harmful effects of the climate, and for you, for the sake of your righteousness, to attain the promised life." As a result, the stork gave them a place. And it happened that when the sparrows raised the chicks, a snake crept in to steal from their number. Seeing this, the stork struck and killed the snake, and he walked around his boundaries, killing all the snakes in order to save them.

Original Moral
This fable teaches us to share the sorrows of the weak, so that, in return for their kindness, we may find salvation in both lives.

156
THE MONKEY AND THE MIRROR
Vardan Aygektsi

The monkey wanted to look at itself in the mirror, and wandering around in search of it, entered a latrine[31], looked down, saw herself and laughed. "Such a face, like mine," she said, "needs such a mirror; this is what suits me."

Original Moral
The fable shows that every person, whether they are weak or powerless, must know their limit, as the monkey realized its ugliness.

---

[31] A latrine is a basic, outdoor facility with a trench or pit where people would relieve themselves.

It's time.
Your eyes should take a break.
Engage your brilliant mind instead.
You know the drill,
There is a page with ink to fill…

157
THE VILLAGE OF ASTRAY
Vardan Aygektsy

Someone was on his way to a village called Astray, but he lost his way. He met another man and asked him, "My friend, how do I get to Astray?" The other man replied, "Brother, leave the path and no matter where you go, you will always end up going astray[32]."

Modern Insight
We rely heavily on our rational mind to make decisions ignoring the power of our feelings and emotions. Remember, our hearts can guide us towards the right path and help us make decisions that align with our true desires and values. When lost or off track, listen to your heart and make changes accordingly, as your feelings are often the best indicator of what is right for you.

---

[32] This fable contains a play on words, with the village name of Astray, which means crooked, incorrect, or awry. The moral of the story is that once you go astray, you will always be on the wrong path, no matter where you go.

158
THE POOR MAN AND THE GOLDEN EGG-LAYING TURKEY
Vardan Aygektsi

A poor man had many sons, and God gave him a turkey that laid a golden egg every day. This was enough for them to live their daily needs. But the poor man grew greedy and said, "I'll kill this bird, take out the gold it has in reserve, and become rich." When he killed the bird, he found in its stomach the same thing that is found in other birds, and he lost a small income.

Original Moral
The fable shows that anyone who desires greatness, inappropriate and disproportionate for them, and reaches out with greed, will lose what they have.

159
THE FOX AND THE CROW WITH CHEESE
Vardan Aygektsy

The crow was near starvation, so she went and stole a little cheese from a farmer and came back with it to sit on the highest rock to eat it. But at the base of the rock was a fox. She saw the crow with cheese in its mouth and began to flatter her, saying, "Glory to the living God! Where did this dazzling sun come from? It is beautiful and like the moon; its face is holy, and its feathers shine like stars. If I had known that its voice was powerful, I would have anointed it king of the world." The crow was flattered by the false praise and forgot about the cheese, and thought to itself, "If I am so beautiful, then my voice must be powerful as well." She spread her wings and loudly cawed once: the cheese fell out and fell to the fox. Then the fox said to the crow, "Yes, your voice is good, and you have more than enough reasons to rule; only you have no sense. You couldn't even keep a piece of cheese, and how will you keep a kingdom?"

Modern Insight
The temptation of flattery can be irresistible, so remember to stay grounded in reality. Be aware of your own abilities and accomplishments, and don't let the sweet words lead you astray.

160
THE JACKDAW[33] IN STRANGER'S FEATHERS
Vardan Aygektsi

The birds gathered together and decided to visit Aramazd, hoping to crown the most beautiful among them as their king. A black-feathered jackdaw collected feathers that had fallen from other birds while they bathed and adorned herself with them, giving her a magnificent appearance. Impressed, Aramazd crowned her as the king. However, when the birds took flight, the borrowed feathers fell from the jackdaw and she was left with her natural black feathers once again.

Modern Insight
The fable reminds us that trying to be someone else can never lead to true success and happiness. Embrace your uniqueness and find your own path in life, rather than imitating others. It's a challenging task, but the rewards of true fulfillment and living an authentic life are immeasurable.

---

[33] A jackdaw is a bird species in the crow family, Corvidae. It is a small to medium-sized bird, with distinctive black feathers on the head and neck, and iridescent blue and purple feathers on the back and wings.

161
THE PRINCE AND THE FISH
Vardan Aygektsi

A certain prince went to the beach where there was a gathering of many fish. He began to have fun and rejoice and called the fish with the words, "Come out of the sea, come to me rejoicing, it's time to listen to me." The fish did not listen at all and did not come out of the sea for the games. Then the prince ordered the fishermen, "Extract them." Pulling the fishing net, they brought them to the shore, and the fish began to flop and struggle from side to side, as their breath was spiraling. But the prince said, "Pitiful fish, now it's useless for you to be playful, because the day is already leaning towards evening, and when I called, you did not come."

162
PARTRIDGE
Vardan Aygektsi

A partridge steals the egg of another partridge and puts it in her nest. When she hatches the chicks, the chick that hatched from the stolen egg, upon hearing the mother's voice, leaves the one who stole it and goes to its own mother.

Modern Insight
No matter where life takes us, our family is always our anchor. Though we may not choose them, they are the ones who will always be there for us through thick and thin. Family is our constant source of love, support, and comfort. It's where we can always go to find a sense of belonging and refuge during difficult times. Cherish your family, as they are the ones who will always have your back.

163
THE SICK LION AND THE HEARTLESS AND EARLESS DONKEY
Vardan Aygektsi

The lion fell ill and the doctors said that there is only one cure for this illness - to boil the heart and ears of the donkey and have the lion drink the broth, and then he will recover. They called the fox and said, "Can you bring a donkey?" "Okay," she said, "I know an extremely plump donkey, my blood brother, who lives in a certain canyon." The fox went to the donkey and said, "Good brother, you are blessed because I have found your elder brother who wants to see you. He is the king, and you will rule with him." The donkey believed and went to see the lion. The lion wanted to suffocate the donkey, but the donkey ran away. The fox caught up with him and said, "Why are you running away?" The donkey said, "The lion nearly strangled me when he kissed me." "That's a sign of strong love," the fox teased, "so if you kiss him again, you'll have fun." The donkey went back to kiss the lion, and, grabbing him by the neck, the lion killed him and walked away to rest. Then the fox took out the heart and ears of the donkey and ate them, saying, "If this is a medicine, it's more useful to me than to the lion." She went to the doctor and the lion and said, "Wonderful, it turns out that the donkey has neither a heart, nor ears." When they arrived and saw that indeed, he had no heart or ears, everyone was surprised, and the fox said, "Don't be surprised, if he had a heart or ears, he wouldn't have come back and thrown himself into your embrace to die after hearing your roar and escaping from your hands."

164
THE FOX AND THE WOLF
Vardan Aygektsi

The fox spotted cheese in a trap, went to the wolf, and said, "Go ahead, brother, take the cheese and eat it. I'm abstaining from food today because it's Friday." The wolf came over with a grin and attempted to grab the cheese, but the trap snapped shut and the cheese fled away. The fox caught it and started munching on it. The wolf said, "Oh sister, what a shame! It's Friday today, don't eat the cheese or else you'll anger God." The fox replied, "It's not me that's facing God's wrath, it's you who's in trouble because today is Friday." The wolf became nervous, twitching back and forth. The fox said, "I was in the same boat once, but I couldn't save myself." The wolf sighed, "Woe is me, I'm in so much pain!" The fox warned, "That's not the end yet, brother. Just wait until the owner of the trap arrives."

Modern Insight
When someone has a history of lying and deceit, it is best to keep your distance and avoid getting involved with them. Trust is a valuable and fragile thing, and once it is broken, it can be difficult, if not impossible, to restore. It's important to surround yourself with trustworthy people and build relationships based on honesty and integrity.

165
THE FOX AND THE EAGLE
Vardan Aygektsi

The fox and the eagle made a pact, agreed to bring their prey to one place and then eat it together. When the fox hunted, the eagle would come and they would eat the prey together. But when the eagle hunted, he would take the prey and sit on high trees and cliffs so that the fox couldn't reach it. The fox realized the eagle's deceit and said, "Brother, you turn out to be a rogue, cunning, and greedy."

Original Moral
The parable shows that a person should live a truthful life and avoid deceit and hypocrisy in their relationship with others.

Modern Insight
Always be honest and transparent in partnerships, and uphold your end of the agreement. If you break your word or deceive your partner, the relationship will suffer and may even end. Your word is your bond, and it is a reflection of your character and values.

166
THE BOY AND THE CHICKEN
Vardan Aygektsi

A woman went to the garden to pick fruit and told her son, "Child, don't take your eyes off the chicks and guard them while I'm gone." The boy got up, tied the chicks with a rope, attached the end of the rope to the leg of the hen, and started playing. And then the hawk appeared and grabbed one of the chicks, and the mother and all the chicks were pulled along.

Modern Insight
Laziness, as well as careless and thoughtless actions can lead to unintended and disastrous consequences. It's important to think before acting, be responsible and attentive to our tasks, especially when entrusted with the safety and well-being of others.

167
THE ANT AND THE DOVE
Vardan Aygektsi

An ant fell into the water and was drowning. A dove appeared and threw a branch into the water. The ant climbed onto it and revived. Just then, a birdcatcher spread his net and was about to catch the dove. The ant crawled up the birdcatcher's leg and bit him at the top of the thigh. The birdcatcher suddenly jumped from the pain and scratched himself: the reed and the net shook, and the dove flew away and escaped.

Modern Insight
Be kind towards others.
Do good deeds and help those in need whenever possible. By acting in such a way you sow seeds of positivity and kindness that may come back to you unexpectedly.

168
THE ANTS AND THE TREES
Vardan Aygektsi

The ants made an alliance with the wooden tribes, promising to burn with them in fire, and then the trees gave them a dwelling place in their hollows, cracks, and indentations.

Modern Insight
Sometimes, in order to survive, we must make alliances with those who are stronger than us, even if the terms are not ideal. It's important not to hesitate due to the uncertainties of the future. Thoroughly evaluate your options and act decisively, for indecision itself is a decision, one that carries its own set of consequences.

169
PATRIOTISM OF THE FROGS
Vardan Aygektsi

In the tiniest spring ponds, frogs were born and raised. When the water started to dry up, the frogs that lived in the river came to them and begged, "Come to our immortal waters - pity yourself, for your water has dried up from the sun's scorching heat." They replied, "We cannot abandon our homeland." The water soon ran out, and the frogs perished.

Modern Insight
Stay in your comfort zone long enough, and you might fail to recognize when it is time to move on or make a change. Be bold, open-minded, and flexible to change. Let go of old ways and embrace new opportunities when the chance presents them to you.

170
THE ANT-LION
Vardan Aygektsi

In an uninhabited, far-off desert lives an ant the size of a sheep. The lion mates with it, and the ant gives birth to an offspring that is half lion, half ant, and people call it "ant-lion". It goes to its mother and cannot eat her food - grain, because it has a lion's body. Then it goes to its father and cannot eat his food - meat, because it has an ant's body. During this journey from one to the other, it perishes from hunger, as it is written in the Scriptures: the ant-lion died from lack of food.

Modern Insight

Attempting to fit into two different worlds to which you seemingly belong can lead to disappointment and failure. Instead, embrace your true nature and identity by looking within to understand who you really are. Use this understanding as a starting point to bravely pave your path towards success and prosperity.

171
THE KING, THE DOG, AND THE SHADOW
Vardan Aygektsi

Once, a king was resting on the delightful bank of a river and a dog, worn out with hunger, was nearby. Upon seeing it, the king threw a beautiful loaf of bread to the dog. The dog took the bread in its mouth and turned down along the river. It stopped at the edge of the river and, upon looking down, saw its shadow - a dog with bread in its mouth. Overcome with greed, the dog lost its mind and forgot about the bread it was holding. It ran to the river barking and tried to grab the bread that it saw in its shadow's mouth. But in the process, it dropped the bread from its own mouth into the river. The dog went down to the bottom of the river but did not find the bread because it was only a shadow. Emerging from the river empty-handed, the dog cried bitterly because it had lost both the bread it had held and the bread it had seen in its shadow's mouth. Finally, exhausted from hunger, it died.

Modern Insight
Being greedy can lead to losing what you already possess. Be content with what you have and avoid coveting the possessions of others. Neglect this advice, and you may lose even what you already have.

172
THE DRAGONFLY AND THE BEE
Vardan Aygektsi

The dragonfly came to the bee and cried, pleading with her, "Have mercy on me in the name of God, because now it is winter, a difficult time, and here I am dying of hunger." The bee said to her, "Tell me, what were you doing during the summer time, that you did not gather food for yourself?" The dragonfly said, "What can I say? I am ashamed! In the summer, I had a wedding feast every day and had fun sitting on tall, beautiful trees and entertaining all passersby with songs to the extreme." The bee said, "So you die a deserved death from hunger, you lazy worker!" and drove her away.

Modern Insight
Posh life, laziness, and negligence are short-lived. Hard work, diligence, and careful planning create a foundation for success and prosperity.

173
THE AGING LION AND THE FOX
Olympian

The cunning lion, whose strength and dominance were lost to old age, employed his wit to make hunting easier. He feigned illness and expressed his misfortune, drawing animals to him from all directions. Upon receiving them, the lion carried out his familiar practice of preying upon them. However, the clever fox saw through the lion's ploy. She approached from the outside, remaining at the door and greeting the lion from there. The lion asked, "Why are you the only one standing outside the doors?" The fox replied, "These tracks hold me back, as I can see the tracks of those who have entered, but not yet the tracks of those who have left."

Original Moral
Deceiving the unwary with cunning is all too common, but the wise are not easily fooled.

174
THE CROW AND THE SWAN
Olympian

The crow was unhappy with her appearance and wished to be white like the swan. "It's no wonder there's such a difference," the swan said, "you've tarnished your wings by lingering around altars in smoky air, while I am surrounded by lush meadows and sparkling rivers." The crow, thinking that the swan had told the truth, left and dragged herself through the rivers and marshes in the hope of transforming her wings; but, overcome by hunger and cold, she withered, and the blackness did not decrease at all.

Original Moral
It's not wise to adopt a new appearance that goes against one's natural image.

Modern Insight
Find contentment in who you are, and never compare yourself to others. Attempting to mold yourself into an idealized standard will ultimately result in dissatisfaction. Embrace and acknowledge your authentic qualities and strengths instead.

175
THE YOUNG BULLS AND THE LION
Olympian

Three young bulls grazed together, and there was a lion nearby. Out of fear for him, the young bulls armed themselves with love and agreement, and together they went out for anything, together they went to pasture, and together they prepared defense against the lion. Then the lion, unable to break their power with strength or cunning, tamed them: under the guise of friendship, he approached each of them separately, passed on mutual gossip, and, turning them into enemies and dividing them, he took possession of them.

Modern Insight
Unity is a strength. Division is a weakness. Strong teams stay united to succeed and achieve great things. Gossip and divisive behavior can erode even the strongest alliances. Keep these negative elements out of the team dynamic to maintain unity and maximize success.

176
THE MONKEYS BUILDING A CITY
Olympian

The monkeys decided to do something beyond their nature. They envied humans and decided to settle in a city, establish assemblies and sites for discussions, teach sciences, and live a human life. When this idea was expressed and the works began, the oldest of them said, "Why the fuss? Nowadays, it's hard for people to catch us, but once we are inside the fence, they will easily surround and hunt us down."

Modern Insight
Try to be something you are not, go beyond your nature, and you'll be on your way to disgrace. Embrace and appreciate your unique qualities, and don't try to imitate. Envy and desire can lead to a downfall.

177
THE MOON AND THE SUN
Unknown Author

The Moon said to the Sun, "I am your child. Sew a dress for me!" The Sun replied, "What size should I make the dress when you don't stay the same size even for one day?"

Modern Insight
Adapting to constant change is a challenge. Keep an open mind, go with the flow, and embrace change to cope gracefully. Remain fixed and rigid, and be prepared for frustration and failure.

178
THE EAGLE, THE PARTRIDGE AND THE ANT
Olympian

The partridge sought help from the ant while being chased by the eagle. Despite the ant's appeal on her behalf, the eagle ignored their plea. The ant, feeling angry, sought revenge. She climbed up to the eagle's nest, knocked out the eggs, and long deprived the eagle of offspring. The eagle flew away and placed its egg in the king's lap. The ant then approached the king, wormed its way between his legs, and bit him in the thigh. The king jumped in pain, causing the eagle's egg to fall and shatter.

Original Moral
This tale illustrates the importance of not making an enemy of anyone, no matter how poor or weak they may seem.

Modern Insight
Every person possesses a particular quality or attribute that it excels in, no matter how weak they may appear. Refrain from creating enemies, regardless of their size or circumstances. Instead, focus on cultivating friendships. It will prove to be a more worthwhile investment.

179
THE EAGLE AND THE OWL[34]
Aesop / Vardan Aygektsi

Once upon a time, a herd of sheep were grazing in a field when an eagle suddenly appeared and carried away one of the lambs. The eagle flew into the sky, and disappeared. An owl was sitting nearby and saw how the eagle stole the lamb. The owl was envious of the eagle and thought to himself, "I'm stronger than the eagle, my claws are thicker than his. Why can't I take a sheep, if the eagle took a lamb?" The owl encouraged himself and flew over the herd of sheep, trying to grab a sheep with his claws, but he failed. His claws got tangled in the sheep's wool and the owl hung from the sheep's back. A shepherd came along, broke the owl's bones with his staff, killed him, tied his legs, put him over his shoulder, and went home with the sheep. When the villagers saw what the shepherd was carrying, they asked, "What is that on your shoulder?" The shepherd replied, "It's an animal that thought it was an eagle, but to us, it's just an owl."

Original Moral
This fable teaches us to be content with what we have and not to reach for what is beyond our grasp, otherwise, we may end up as a laughingstock like the owl, and even lose our life.

---

[34] N. Marr suggests that this fable originates from the collection of Aesop's fables. However, it also appears in one of Armenian fable anthologies, indicating it may have been adapted into Armenian under Vardan's authorship.

180
THE ROOSTER, THE FOX AND THE DOG
Aesop/Armenian version

A rooster was loudly praying and shouting on a tree branch. A fox came along and asked him to come down, saying, "We don't have a philosopher[35] with us today, and it's the feast of Saint Karapet. Let's celebrate together." The rooster replied, "Just a minute, let me wait for my uncle so we can celebrate properly." In the morning, a hunting dog appeared and grabbed the fox by the throat. The fox started making wheezing, unpleasant noises. The rooster sadly said, "Oh no, what an unpleasant voice you wanted to use to celebrate the feast of the blessed Saint Karapet."

Original Moral
The moral of the story is: if you try to trick someone, you'll end up falling into the trap you set for them.

---

[35] In Armenian culture, the title of "philosopher" was awarded to exceptional teachers of religious singing.

181
THE BIRDCATCHER AND THE FALCON
Unknown Author

A story is told about a birdcatcher who used to catch birds in a trap, and whenever he caught one, he would let it go. One day, a falcon got caught. But the birdcatcher quickly put him in a cage and closed the door tightly. Then the falcon asked the birdcatcher, "Oh man, why did you release all the birds when you caught them, but when you caught me, you quickly put me in a cage?" The birdcatcher said, "Oh falcon, I was using the birds I caught as bait to catch you in the end."

Modern Insight

Have a clear, long-term vision and a well-thought-out plan in place to achieve your goals. If needed, make small sacrifices or compromises along the way to ultimately reach your desired destination. Patience, persistence, resourcefulness, and adaptability are your best friends on this journey.

182
THE CRANE - THE KING OF BIRDS
Unknown Author

The birds gathered and decided, "We'll appoint as our king the one with the strongest voice, so that he can call us to battle when needed." The crane rose high up and croaked. The birds approved and anointed him as king. The donkey came and said, "See, if you build something for me to stand on and elevate me to the place of the crane, you'll hear whose voice is stronger."

Original Moral
The moral of the story is: no matter how weak and poor a person may be, he can govern the state if the people and the army have approved him and made him king.

183
THE FOX AND THE STORK
Armenian Folk Fable

The fox and the stork became friends. Both built their nests in the same place and had offspring. Both hunted and brought food for their children. The fox strangled the stork's chicks every day and fed them to her own offspring. When all the chicks were gone, the fox told the stork, "The kids are disappearing, my friend." The stork asked, "Mine or yours?" The fox said, "Both mine and yours." The stork asked, "The long-necked or the short ones?" The fox said, "The long-necked ones." The stork said, "Oh, cunning fox."

Modern Insight
Remember that not everyone can be trusted. Always be vigilant and cautious of those who may not have your best interests at heart. Ask questions to expose the deceitful nature of people, and never let anyone take advantage of you.

184
THE SNAKE AND THE FARMER
Unknown Author

The snake became friends with the farmer. When they reached a river, the farmer placed the snake in his bosom and they crossed the river, but the snake did not want to get out. They went to many judges but none of them settled their dispute. They came to the fox and said, "Judge us." The fox understood what the matter was and said, "I can't judge you from a distance, you snake, come out of the farmer's bosom, stand face to face and tell your case!" When the snake came out of the farmer's bosom and stood on its tail, the fox signaled the farmer, "Hit her with the staff that you have in your hand!" He killed the snake with a blow and she started wriggling. The fox approached, straightened the snake with her paw and said, "Can you hold yourself straight like this?"

Original Moral
This fable teaches an important lesson about the dangers of forming alliances with deceitful people for personal gain. It also emphasizes the importance of authority figures, such as judges, kings, elders, and other influential people, in correcting the behavior of wicked and cunning individuals.

185
THE WISE JUDGE
Vardan Aygektsi

It is said in fables that two very friendly men went on a trip and one lost a lot in trade, while the other became successful. They returned home and, upon arrival, approached their city. The poor man said to his rich companion, "Brother, I have experienced a lot of kindness and love from you, but the most important thing is what I will ask of you and what would be above all: I need you to be a good friend to me and give me a loan of a thousand drams, so that this year I can satisfy the needs of my home and my children, and next year, on this very day, I will return the money to you. Consider that you are redeeming my children from captivity for the sake of your soul." And the rich friend, hearing this, with a pure heart gave him a thousand drams, sympathizing with his poverty. And, leaving there, they each went home. When the year was up, the one who gave the money went to the debtor and said, "The year is up, now give me back the money so I can use it for the needs of my home and my children." The other responded, "I owe you no money." When he started to insist, he said, "Let's go to the judge." And when they arrived, the judge said to them, "Did you borrow money from him or not?" And to the other, "Do you have a witness and a receipt?" When the judge learned that there was no receipt and no witness, he said to the one who gave the money, "Was there anyone nearby when you gave him the money, or was there any livestock, or a horse?" The one who gave the money said, "There was no one nearby: above was God, and below were the two of us! He begged me, I took pity and gave it to him, and now he denies it!" The judge said, "Was there a tree, a bush, a stone? What kind of place was it?" The owner of the money said, "There was no tree or bush: it was at the foot of a cliff, we sat there, I counted the money and gave it to him, and, leaving from there, we both came to the city together, he went home and I went home!" The judge said to the owner of the money, "Can you bring that rock here or break off a piece of it and bring it?" The loaner, who was anxious about getting his money back, ran out thinking, "I'll go, I'll drag that rock with a thousand horses, or break it and bring a fragment." And when he left, the judge asked the other man who stayed with him, "Can he move the rock from its place or break it and bring a piece?" The man who denied the debt said, "Even if he hitches a thousand horses, he can't move the rock from its place, and if he brings a thousand stonemasons, he can't break off a piece, because it's a solid rock." Then the judge brought back the man who left and said to the one who denied the debt, "Go and give him his money, because you yourself are a witness that you owe him." And so, being ashamed, he paid his debt.

Original Moral
This fable shows that a judge must be such that, when rendering judgment, he can find a solution to any case.

136

186
MISADVENTURES OF THE WOLF
Vardan Aygektsi

Once upon a time, a wolf grabbed a lamb and wanted to eat it. The lamb asked the wolf, "Oh wolf, I have heard that wolves have beautiful voices and are great trumpet players. I have a long-standing desire to hear your voice. If you're going to eat me, can you play a tune on your trumpet first so I can hear it?" The wolf, believing the lamb, stood on his hind legs, put his front paws to his mouth, and howled. The sound woke up the dogs, who surrounded the wolf and started to attack him. The wolf barely escaped and the lamb was saved. The wolf, wounded, went to the mountains and saw two flocks of wild sheep grazing. Two sheep approached the wolf, one from each flock, and said, "Oh wolf, we fight each other every day. If we graze on this side, they say it's their pasture, and if we go to the other side, we fight again. Please divide the field for us so each flock can graze on their own area and we won't fight anymore. And from each flock, we will give you one yearling ewe[41] for you to eat." The wolf agreed, wagged his tail, and started to make marks with his tail. But suddenly, both sheep charged at the wolf, trying to tear open his belly with their horns. The wolf barely escaped. The wolf, hungry and wounded, went to a valley where there was a mill. The door was open and the cat was sitting in the doorway, washing itself. The wolf saw the cat and thought he could catch it. But the cat ran inside the mill and the wolf followed, pushing the door shut behind him. The cat escaped through a window, leaving the wolf trapped inside. The wolf thought to himself, "What a fool I am. Was anyone in my family a singer or trumpet player that I howled? That's why the dogs woke up and tried to

---

[41] Yearling ewe refers to a female sheep that is one year old.

tear my belly open. And what makes me think I can divide areas for wild sheep? Their horns were ready to stab into my belly. And now I've trapped myself in the mill. If the miller comes now, he'll grab me by the tail and drag me back and forth until my tail is in his hand." Just then, the miller came and saw the wolf in the corner of the mill. He took a stick and started beating the wolf so badly that the wolf didn't know how to escape. The wolf hung his head in the water hole, trying to escape, but the miller grabbed him by the tail and wouldn't let go. The wolf tried to escape, but his tail remained in the miller's hand while he fell into the gutter and escaped through the water hole. The wolf, wounded, walked down a path through a garden where a scholar was sitting and reading the Quran while rocking back and forth over the book. The wolf asked the scholar, "Oh scholar, what are you reading?" The scholar replied, "What am I to read? I am seeking the fulfillment of my desire." The wolf said, "If you want your wish to come true, stand up and go to the mill. Speak your wish there, and before the words are even off your lips, it will be granted."

187
THE WOLF, THE FOX AND THE MULE
Vardan Aygektsi

The wolf, fox, and mule went together and when they became hungry and no food was found, they said, "Let's eat the one among us who is younger." This was said by the wolf and the fox, as they wanted to eat the mule. The wolf was asked, "How old are you, wolf?" He said, "I am the wolf whom Noah took in the ark." The fox stepped forward and said, "You're ten generations younger than me: I am that fox which God created." The mule stepped forward, and it was a new moon, and said, "My birth year is recorded on my hoof, come and read how old I am." He raised his leg. The fox said to the wolf, "I know you went to school, come and read this inscription." The wolf believed and approached to read. The mule said, "Come closer, it's a small inscription." The wolf approached even closer, and the mule hit the wolf very hard, breaking his skull, and the wolf ran away with a roar. The fox said to the wolf, "Go, there's another line even smaller, read it." The wolf said, "How would I know how to read? We are butchers and the offspring of butchers from generation to generation."

Original Moral
This fable shows that anyone who leaves their trade, which they learned and studied, and goes to do what they have not studied and don't know, will break their head like the wolf, because everyone should do what they have learned.

188
SHAH ABBAS, THE JUG OF WINE AND THE MIDDLEMAN
Unknown Author

Once upon a time, King Shah Abbas[37] was riding his horse through the city when a drunk man stopped him and asked, "How much for your horse? I want to buy it." Realizing that the man was not in his right mind, the king ordered his men to take the drunkard home and bring him back the next day when he was sober. The next morning, the man was filled with regret and fear, but his clever wife gave him a jug of wine and taught him what to say. When he was brought before the king again, Shah Abbas asked, "So, how much were you willing to pay for my horse?" The man took out the jug of wine and placed it in front of the king, saying, "Your Majesty, I am but a humble middleman. This is the one who was interested in purchasing your horse. If you wish to discuss the price, you can speak directly with him. And if you like, you can pay me a small middleman's fee." Impressed by the man's clever response, the king rewarded him and allowed to go free.

Modern Insight
A sharp mind is worth more than a jug of wine.
Don't let alcohol cloud your judgment, or you may end up trying to buy the king's horse.

---

[37] Shah Abbas of Persia, also known as Abbas the Great, was the fifth Safavid Shah of Iran, ruling from 1588 until his death in 1629. He is widely regarded as one of the most influential monarchs in Iranian history and is credited with modernizing the country's military, economy, and culture.

189
THE WEALTHY MAN AND HIS TWO SONS
Unknown Author

Once upon a time, there lived a wealthy man who had two sons. He possessed two types of treasures: one that was well-known to everyone and another that he kept secret. The man decided to distribute his known wealth among his sons, but he chose to keep the secret treasure undisclosed. Then, he embarked on a journey and gradually spent all that he had, leaving himself in a state of poverty. After some time, wanting to test his sons, he returned to them, seeking their assistance. One of his sons, lacking compassion, scolded the man, while the other son, filled with love and generosity, shared everything he had with his seemingly destitute father. Discovering the true nature of his sons, the father shared the sacred treasure with the compassionate son, while letting the other son go.

Modern Insight
True wealth is not measured by material possessions, but by the richness of one's heart. Those who show kindness, generosity, and compassion in the face of adversity are the ones deserving of the greatest rewards.

*You're almost done. Reflect, then write.
Noteworthy lessons or insights?*

190
THE KING OF BABYLON AND THE OLD MAN
Unknown Author

As the King of Babylon made his entrance into a city, heading his immense army, he spotted an elderly man diligently planting a date tree. Struck by curiosity, he approached the man and asked, "My good man, why are you wasting your time planting this tree? It won't bear fruit for another forty years, a time you may not live to witness." The old man replied, "Your Majesty, I have enjoyed the fruits of a tree planted by someone else all my life. I am planting this tree now so that someone else might enjoy its bounty." The king declared, "Award him a thousand dahekans, for his kindness is a virtue to be celebrated."

Modern Insight
The true measure of our life is not its duration, but the impact we make through our actions and contributions. Though our physical presence may be fleeting, the legacy we leave behind - much like the timeless works of renowned composers, artists and writers - ensures our spirit lives on.

191
THE SEA FROGS
Mkhitar Gosh

The sea frogs gathered for a council and said, "Why are we drowning in the water with bloated bellies and yellow skin? Let's go ashore and live like everyone else." One of the elders said, "My father counseled me to never leave the sea's sanctuary because, by our nature, we are timid. We might venture out and then turn back in fear, revealing our timidity." But they didn't heed his advice and emerged onto the land. However, upon hearing footsteps, they fled and plunged back into the sea.

Original Moral
As wisdom tells us in a proverb: one must first recognize one's capabilities before changing one's location or job.

192
THE LION, THE BEAR, AND THE WOLF
Mkhitar Gosh

Once upon a time, a lion, a bear, and a wolf became friends and proclaimed, "Why must we remain carnivores? Let us catch a human who can prepare meals from our hunted prey according to their customs." And so, they did, capturing a man to act as their cook. The man, disheartened, began to plot his escape. He split a large log, inserting wedges on either side, and said to the lion and the others, "Help me split this log. Insert your paws into the crack and pull." As soon as they did, he pulled out the wedges, trapping the beasts. Then, seizing an axe, he prepared to dispatch them, declaring, "We shall start with the lion."

Modern Insight
Even the strongest can be outwitted by cleverness and quick thinking.

193
THE REPENTANT WOLF
Mkhitar Gosh

An old wolf approached a herd and proclaimed, "I have seen the error of my ways, and I am deeply sorry for the distress I have caused. Therefore, I wish to join you and serve as a gatekeeper in your home, seeking forgiveness, and to protect your young ones from other wolves." Overjoyed, the herd told their guard dogs, "Do not bother him anymore." The wolf waited until the lambs had grown, then he began eating and devouring them, until the majority noticed and put an end to him.

Modern Insight
Beware of the sly fox changing its coat; old habits die hard, and trust is to be earned, not freely given.

194
THE WISE JUDGE
Vardan Aygektsi

There was a man with a spiteful wife, and she picked a fight with him, exclaiming, "Do you think all three of your sons are yours? Only one of them is, the other two aren't." When he asked which one was his, she refused to reveal. As the man lay on his deathbed, he declared, "All my wealth shall go to my true son." After his death, the brothers quarreled amongst themselves. Each claimed to be the true son and rightful heir to the wealth. Unable to settle the dispute, they sought the counsel of a wise judge. The judge ordered them to exhume their father's body and shoot an arrow into it. He who would strike his father with an arrow, and the arrow would pierce his father's body, he would be the true son. Two of the sons shot arrows at their father's body, but the true son pulled out a knife to kill his brothers, and cried bitter tears, burying his father's body. And they knew then that he was the true son, and gave him his father's wealth.

Modern Insight
Genuine connection and kinship are proven by our actions during times of trial, not by our words or our entitlements.

195
WINE
Vardan Aygektsi

There was a king who had a son, and he commanded his ministers to carry his son and pay him respect every day. And they did as commanded. One day, a minister was set to honor the royal son and took him to the royal house in the evening, then left. The prince had drunk heavily and walked out drunk, fell into a garbage heap, and died. The king then ordered that during his reign, all vineyards should be closed and wine jars be smashed. And so, it was done. There was a widow who had a son, and she didn't destroy her barn and wine and every morning and evening, she gave her son two cups of wine with bread. One night, the widow's son went out, killed the king's lion, and the king commanded in the morning that whoever killed my lion, if he comes and tells me, I will not punish him. The widow came with her son. The king asked him how he had killed the lion. The son said that he had gone out at night, encountered the lion, and killed it. His mother added that she had nourished him with wine, and explained how she had done so. Then, the king issued a decree: vineyards were to be planted and wine consumed in such a manner that could enable one to slay a lion rather than die in a rubbish heap.

Modern Insight
A moderate bit of wine might empower you to slay a lion, but overdoing it could land you in a heap of trouble - quite literally! So remember, one glass may make you bold, two will do the trick, but with three you might just kick the bucket in a rubbish bin!

196
THE KING AND THE SNAKE
Vardan Aygektsi

Once upon a time, there lived a king who had a beloved snake that brought him a red dahekan every day. The king had a child whom he fed on the throne, and would drape the snake around the child's neck, and thus the snake and the child would play. As the child grew older, one day during their play, he pulled out his sword, cut off the snake's tail, and threw it on the ground. The snake, enraged, struck the child with its venom, and the child died instantly, and the snake then fled to a foreign land. When the king arrived and saw his child, blackened and dead from the snake's poison, and the snake's tail lying on the ground, he understood that his child had cut off the snake's tail with his sword. He mourned for his son, took him, and buried him in a grave. Time passed, and the king sent messengers to the snake saying, "I know it was my son who started it: he cut off your tail, and you bit him. What's done is done, and you left in vain. Come back, and we will love each other as before, and live together." However, the snake replied, "It's not like that. For I will always be looking at my tail, and you at the grave of your son, meaning our feud will not disappear. It would be best if we stay far from each other to prevent any greater evil from arising between us."

Modern Insight
Once trust is broken and damage is done, it's challenging to repair. A relationship ended on good terms leaves room for potential reconciliation, while one ended in conflict fosters lasting resentment. Always aim to part ways amicably, leaving the door open for future understanding and respect.

197
THE FOOL AND THE WATERMELON
Vardan Aygektsi

There was a naive and foolish man who had just one dahekan. With it, he went to the city to buy a donkey. He went around the city and its market but could not find a donkey for one dahekan. Then, he returned to the market and noticed a large watermelon. Astonished, he asked, "What is this?" The merchants, seeing his foolishness, told him it was an Indian donkey's egg that would hatch a mighty Indian donkey. Feeling joyful, the man gave his dahekan and took the so-called Indian donkey's egg. The merchants instructed him to carry it carefully, lest it broke and the donkey ran away. As the man walked down a steep path with the watermelon in his hand, he slipped. The watermelon slipped from his hand and rolled into the dense forest. Suddenly, a rabbit darted out of the forest and started running away. The man thought the egg had broken and the donkey had escaped. Chasing the rabbit, he yelled, "Hey, Indian donkey, woe is me! Don't run away, please, have pity on me and come back."

Modern Insight
Be wary of those selling "donkey eggs"! Gullibility can make one see donkeys where only rabbits exist. It's better to laugh at oneself than to chase rabbits, calling them donkeys!

198
THE FATHER AND THE SON
Vardan Aygektsi

A man found a suitable woman for his son and arranged their marriage. When the son united with her, he greatly admired the workings of marriage and felt joyous. He started lecturing his father about marital matters. To this, the father replied, "Oh son, I brought you into this world through marriage, and now you are schooling me on it?"

Modern Insight
Just as a chick cannot tutor a hen on egg-laying, wisdom and experience aren't best taught by the novice.

199
THE RULER AND THE WISE MAN
Vardan Aygektsi

Once upon a time, there was a global ruler who had a strikingly handsome son. The ruler declared that he would find a beautiful maiden to be his son's wife, hoping to have equally beautiful grandchildren to inherit his throne. He found a stunning bride for his son. However, before they had any children, the son passed away, leaving the young widow behind. Desiring the widow for himself, the ruler sought the advice of wise men, asking, "Is it permissible?" The wise men told him that a father has no right to marry his daughter-in-law. Unwilling to accept their judgment, the ruler turned to another wise man, who happened to be his favorite. This wise man told the ruler, "In the world, there are seventy-two nations, and it is not permissible for any of them, but it is for you." Puzzled, the ruler asked, "Why is it that it's not permissible for the seventy-two nations of the world, but it is for me?" The wise man responded, "I'm afraid to tell you the reason, as you may kill me." The ruler then swore not to punish him if he revealed the reason. Then, the wise man said, "It's because you are beyond any nation and there is no authority above you, and you can do whatever you wish."

Modern Insight
In any sphere of power, those at the top have the freedom to act within their authority. But, having no one above them, the integrity of their actions is determined not by regulation, but by their character and human decency. Absolute power demands absolute responsibility.

200
THE MOUSE AND THE CAMEL
Vardan Aygektsi

Once upon a time, a mouse was filled with pride, lost its wisdom and let arrogance fill its heart. He approached a camel and said, "Permit me to make my nest in your hoof and live there." The camel replied, "This could harm you because I might accidentally step on you, and you will die." The mouse said, "Your hoof is soft and won't cause me any harm." The camel warned, "All right, you reap what you sow." And the mouse made its home in the camel's hoof. One day, as the camel walked under a heavy burden, it unintentionally stepped on the mouse. The mouse squealed, and fat from its belly seeped out, as the mouse was quite chubby. Seeing this, the camel said, "See, brother, this is what worried you, and it came out of your belly."

Modern Insight
Be aware of the potential consequences of your decisions, especially when ignoring wise counsel. Overconfidence and disregard for danger can lead to one's downfall.

201
TWO ARTISTS
Vardan Aygektsi

Once upon a time, a certain king constructed magnificent gates and desired to adorn them with such paints that were never seen anywhere else. He chose two artists and gave one wall to one and another wall to the other, hanging a curtain between them. Once the artists had finished their work, the king came to look at their accomplishments. He saw that one of them had created a beautiful painting, and it pleased him greatly. But the other artist had not painted anything at all; he had made the wall very beautiful by polishing it better than a mirror. Seeing that he had not drawn anything but only polished, the king was surprised and asked, "What have you done?" The artist replied, "I shall reveal my work." He then drew back the separating curtain, and when the light rose and illuminated the polished wall, the painted wall grew darker, for in the mirror were visible all the images that were painted on the other wall. The king declared, "This one is more beautiful than the other."

Modern Insight
In the realm of mastery, simplicity is the crown jewel. However, it is a jewel earned only after navigating the labyrinth of complexity. Once the superfluous is shed, the essence of beauty is expressed in its purest, simplest form - proving that true brilliance often lies in knowing what to omit.

202
THE WISHES OF THREE PRINCES
Unknown Author

Once upon a time, there was a king who had three sons. One day, unbeknownst to his sons, the king was quietly listening in on their conversation in which they were asking each other, "If you were an animal, which one would you choose to be?" The first prince confidently declared, "Were I not human, I'd choose to be a lion, the king of the beasts and a ruthless predator." The second prince claimed, "I'd be an eagle, for it is a ruthless hunter and soars above all others." The third prince said, "I would like to be a dove, for it is innocent and harmless, and it symbolizes peace." Listening to their responses, the king discerned the character of his sons. He recognized the first prince's ruthlessness, the second's arrogance, and the third's peace-loving nature. Thus, tailoring his teachings for each prince according to their traits, he ultimately selected the peace-loving prince to succeed him as king.

Modern Insight
True leadership and worthiness of succession does not lie in displays of power or ruthlessness, but in the capacity for peace, kindness, and humility. It's the gentle, not the fierce, who often make the most benevolent rulers.

203
THE STORY OF THE GOATS AND THE WOLVES
Vardan Aygketsi

All the goats gathered together and sent a message to the wolf tribe saying, "Why do you maintain an unrelenting hostility towards us? We ask you to make peace with us as kings do with other nations." And the wolves gathered and were filled with great joy and sent a messenger with a long message and many gifts to the goat tribe and said, "We heard of your good intention and thanked God because peace is a great joy. We bring to your wisdom's attention that the cause and the beginning of our conflict and war is the shepherd and the dog, and if you drive them away from our presence, peace will immediately come." The goats listened to this and drove the shepherds and the dogs away. They made a solemn and unbreakable agreement. The goats, going out, wandered carelessly through the mountains and deep valleys, grazing and thanking God. The wolves waited ten days and gathered against the goats and destroyed them all.

Original Moral
It is difficult to establish peace among those whose hearts have hardened by nature into hostility due to the hatred of one people to another, of one race to another and of one person to another. Therefore, it is difficult to establish friendship (love) and peace between them, as we see between the rich and the poor.

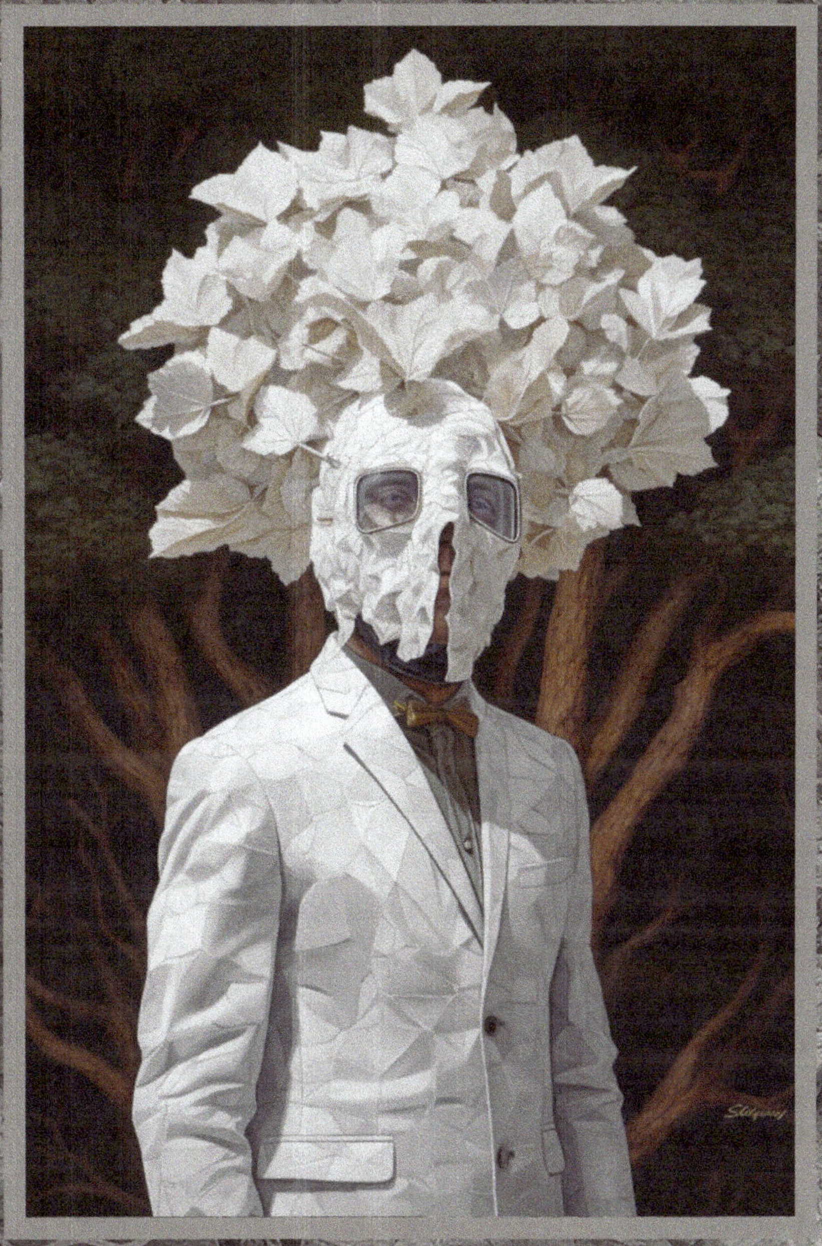

204
THE FOX AND ST. GEORGE
Vardan Aygektsi

The fox crossing the river got caught in a whirlpool and cried, "Hey, St. George! Hey, St. George, hurry! Rescue me from this trouble, and I'll bring you two cups of incense." He hurried and pulled her out. The fox fled the water, and, once the fear passed, went and sat under the rock grumbling, "Look what a disgrace and what an ugliness! While the saints were on earth, in the flesh, they rode on chariots and horses and caused tears to the world. Then once they suffered torture and became pleasing to God, so now they take bribes first and then save a person from trouble." While the fox was speaking, suddenly a dried-up rock trembled and was about to collapse on her. The fox cried out, "Hurry to my help, St. George! I will bring you two cups of incense." St. George took pity on her and saved her again. The fox did not stop talking, went on recklessly, grumbled and said, "Well, here we go again, admire this ugliness. Where do I have incense, to bring it to you, huh, St. George? Am I a merchant, shopkeeper? Well, where do I find incense? I don't have it, and I won't bring it to you." While the fox was talking and grumbling, she suddenly met hunters who released their hounds on her. The fox ran and cried, "Oh, woe, hey, Saint George! Hurry to my help, I went to look for a cup so I could bring you incense, and I'll bring you a lamb too." But he did not come. Dogs caught the fox and chewed her, and so it was. She was howling and crying, "Woe is me, sinful before the saints!" And catching her alive, the dogs skinned her and threw away. And then Saint George appeared to her and said, "Hey, lying dog, you are stained with blood, but you will not be a martyr, you will die in debt."

205
DREAM INTERPRETATION
Mkhitar Gosh

A certain king had a dream in which foxes were falling like rain. The king ordered to announce, "I will give one thousand dahekans to the one who interprets my dream." A poor man heard about this and, appearing, said, "If you give me three days' time, I will explain." The poor man went to the desert and wandered in thought. And there was a snake; seeing the troubled man, he said, "What will you give me if I interpret the king's vision for you?" He answered, "Half of what the king promised me." The snake said to him, "Go and tell the king: the time is coming when people will be treacherous and dishonest, like foxes." He went and said; his words pleased the king, for people were indeed like that, and the king gave the promised thousand coins. But the man cheated the snake and did not return to give him his share. After that, the king had another vision: sheep were falling like rain. And he ordered the same man to interpret this vision, as he had done with the first. The man asked for the same time as before. And he was ashamed to go to the snake again, showing ingratitude, but he still went, scolding himself, and said, "Forgive me, interpret the second vision, and I will pay you for both the first and second interpretation." The snake explained to him, not punishing for the mistake, "Go and announce that the time is approaching and has already come when people will be pure in spirit, like sheep." The man came and gave the interpretation. Approving it, the king again gave a thousand dahekans. Taking them, the man carried the snake a thousand dahekans for the first and second time. After that, the king had another dream: swords were falling like rain. The king again ordered the same man to come and interpret this dream. A man asked for the same term as before and went to the serpent. The snake immediately interpreted his vision as a friend, "Step forward and say: the time has come for people of violence and swords to appear." Arriving, he told the king this, received a thousand dahekans again, and went to the serpent, and spoke for himself, "Why leave the serpent with a thousand dahekans, and bring him another five hundred; I'll strike the snake and kill him." He went to strike the snake, but he couldn't, because the snake escaped from him. And the man repented and thought, "What evil have I done, how will I approach him if I need to again?" Noting that he was upset, the snake told him, "Don't be upset, man, you didn't do anything on your own, you only acted according to the dictate of time. Thus, your deception was at the time of pretenders, your repentance and surrender of a thousand dahekans were at the time of pure-hearted people, and your attempt to strike me was at the time of violent people."

Original Moral
This fable shows that it is necessary to judge people by time and to be cautious, for time gives birth to people of different character, some are cunning, others are pure in spirit, others are tyrants, and many others are similar.

CONTEMPORARY FABLES

M1
THE KING AND THE RUNNING SERVANT
Horizon Avetisyan (circa 1970s)

The king and his entourage were watching the sunset from the balcony, and they saw a caravan passing by the desert in the distance. Curious, the king asked, "I wonder where that caravan is headed?" One of his servants volunteered, "Oh king, let me run and find out." After a while, he returned panting and reported, "My king, the caravan was headed to Tabriz!" The king asked, "And what were they trading?" The servant replied, "My king, let me go and ask them!" So he ran off to catch up with the caravan again and came back out of breath saying, "My king, they were selling figs and dates." The king then asked, "And how much were they selling them for?" "Let me run and find out," said the servant. The king said, "Sit down. You'll die chasing the caravan, because instead of using your wit, you use your feet."

Modern Insight
Wit and forethought can be your most trusted allies in daily tasks. Use your intelligence to solve problems and make decisions, and don't rely on physical attributes alone. Wisdom and resourcefulness are essential characteristics that should be cultivated and used in all aspects of life.

M2
THE SQUIRREL AND THE WOODPECKER
Sar Kamler

The squirrel, noticing how the woodpecker was drilling into the tree to find something to eat, tried to teach him, "Hey, that's not the right way to drill into the wood. You are doing it all wrong. Keep your head up and use the lower part of your beak. You'll be able to do much better." The woodpecker answered, "Thank you, my friend. Have you ever drilled wood yourself?"

Modern Insight
At times, we might feel the need to appear important or knowledgeable by giving advice to others. However, if we lack expertise or knowledge in a certain area, our guidance may not be valuable. It's important to recognize when we don't have the necessary skills or understanding to provide helpful advice and to refrain from doing so. This way, we can avoid potentially harmful or misleading advice and ensure that we only provide guidance when we're qualified to do so.

M3
THE PLUM TREE
Sar Kamler

"It won't become a tree," said the wife skeptically looking at the small seedling that had grown from an unusual spot - a tiny crack between two concrete slabs, "There is no chance it will grow, so you better cut it now." "It will," said the husband. The seedling thrived. It kept consistently growing and in three years it grew into a beautiful plum tree with a slim trunk and small green leaves. "I am wondering when it will give some plums," said the husband. "Not in your lifetime," replied the wife, "Wild-born trees like this don't give fruit." "Let's live and see," said the husband. In the fourth year, the tree produced a bountiful harvest of greenish-yellow oval plums that were sweet as honey.

Modern Insight

Whether the plum tree flourished or not is not important. What truly matters is that it won't hurt to believe in the potential of something, even if it seems improbable or difficult. Disbelief might rob us of incredible opportunities. After all, the most astonishing outcomes often sprout from the seeds of what we initially deemed impossible.

M4
TWO FRIENDS
An Armenian joke

Two childhood friends served together in a war, sharing their bread and fighting side by side. One day, while escaping from the enemy, they found themselves hiding in a basement of a large building. The enemy discovered one friend, but the other remained hidden. As they were taking the captured friend away, he passed by his hidden companion and kicked him, shouting, "Hey, come out, they have caught us."

Modern Insight
Life is unpredictable, but one thing is for sure: the true test of friendship only comes when things get a little 'deathly.'

M5
THE BOWMAN AND THE DOCTOR
Sar Kamler

There was once a hunter who tirelessly hunted for days and nights to provide for his family. One day, he fell gravely ill, and his family called for a doctor. "Take out your bow and pull the string," the doctor instructed the hunter. The bowman pulled the string. "More," said the doctor. The bowman pulled it more. "Even more," said the doctor, "pull with all your might!" "But if I do," gasped the bowman, "it will break apart." "You see," the doctor said, "the same way the human body works. Push it beyond its limits too hard, and it will eventually break apart."

Modern Insight
Take care of yourself so that you can take care of others. Pushing yourself too hard may lead to illness and hinder your ability to provide support. Remember to listen to your body and avoid persistently pushing beyond your limits.

M6
THE SPRUCE AND THE MAGNOLIA
Sar Kamler

Spruce and magnolia trees grew side by side in the same front yard. One spring day, the spruce said to the magnolia, "Your blooms are stunning, but they only last for a short time. You only bloom once a year, while my beauty is year-round." The magnolia replied, "My beauty may be fleeting, but it is highly anticipated. Your beauty may be evergreen, but it's commonplace to the eye."

Modern Insight
When we are surrounded by the same things
day after day, no matter how stunning they may be,
we can become blind to their charms.
Take a break. Step aside. Do something else.
When you return, you'll see with fresh eyes and
appreciate the beauty anew.

M7
TWO FRIENDS
A popular Armenian fable

Once upon a time, two friends went for a walk in the woods. Suddenly, a big bear came out of nowhere and started to chase them. Seeing the bear, one of the friends ran as fast as he could and climbed up a tree, leaving his mate all alone. Knowing he couldn't outrun the bear, the second friend decided to play dead and fell to the ground laying very still. The bear came up, took a sniff, and presuming him dead, went away. Once the danger had passed, the one in the tree descended to his mate and asked, "What did the bear whisper in your ear?" Dusting himself off, his companion replied, "The bear told me that next time, when going for a walk in the woods, I should pick more loyal friends."

Modern Insight
A friend in need is a friend indeed.

M7
THE PAPERWORK
An Armenian joke, retold by Sar Kamler

A wolf decided to open a coffee shop and hired his buddy rabbit as a barista, making him work 12 hours a day with no days off. The poor rabbit was so exhausted that he went to complain to the lion about his inhumane working conditions. The lion stepped in and set the rules that the rabbit would only work on Mondays, Wednesdays, and Fridays. On the first Monday, the wolf approached the rabbit and said, "Hey buddy, I know your shifts changed, but the turtle got sick and can't come to work tomorrow. Could you fill in for him? You can take Wednesday off instead." "Sure," the rabbit replied and the wolf had him fill in a bunch of forms, in case the lion inquired. The next day the wolf approached the rabbit again, "Hey, I know you shouldn't be working tomorrow, but the squirrel is getting married and she can't come on Wednesday. Could you help us and work tomorrow instead of Friday?" "OK," said the rabbit, filling in a stack of papers again. The next day, the wolf asked the rabbit to work instead of the next Monday, and so it continued for the next few weeks. Each time, he made the rabbit deal with piles of paperwork to ensure his own protection. One day, the lion was out for a walk in the park with his wife and spotted the rabbit sitting on a bench, looking gloomy and smoking a cigarette. "Hey buddy," said the lion, "I see the new work shift is working out for you! Are you enjoying your time off?" The rabbit replied, "Not exactly, sir. I work pretty much the same as before, except I also have to do a heap of paperwork now!"

M8
THE OLD WOMAN AND HER GOAT
A.Kamalyants (1907)

Once upon a time, there lived an elderly woman who owned a single goat. The milk from this goat was her only means of sustenance. Lacking fodder, she would let her goat graze freely in the nearby fields each morning. As she did, she would say a prayer, "Dear Saint Kirakos, I am a humble woman with little means. Please watch over my goat today and ensure it returns safely this evening." Each day, she would address her plea to a different saint, promising to light a candle in their honor, until one day, on the eve of Christmas, she realized she had appealed to all the saints, angels, and archangels she knew. In her dilemma over who to entrust her goat to, an idea sparked in her mind. "Oh, revered saints, angels of peace in the world! On this blessed day, I entrust my lone goat to you all. Please show mercy on this old woman, protect my goat, and ensure it returns unharmed by nightfall." After this heartfelt prayer, she let her goat out and busied herself with household chores. As dusk approached, she eagerly awaited the return of her goat. But alas, her goat never came back from the fields. Sleepless and distraught, she went to the church at dawn and prayed, "My Lord, I am lost. When I entrusted my goat to a single saint, it was always safe. Yesterday, with high hopes, I entrusted my goat to all the saints, and my goat is missing. I seek fairness. Please, my Lord, judge between me and the saints." Suddenly, an angel appeared before her and said, "Hey grandma, sorry about your loss, but here's what happened. When you entrusted all of us with the protection of your goat, every saint was eager to fulfill this duty. A meeting was called to decide who should undertake the task. As every saint was keen on assuming the responsibility themselves, a dispute started and lasted quite a while. The issue remained unresolved by nightfall.

Just then, a wolf happened to pass by the field, spotted your unguarded goat, and ate it."

Modern Insight
Just as a meeting of saints can end up as a wolf's dinner, so too can office meetings that go on and on without clear purpose or direction. Remember, while you're busy discussing who should do the work, the 'goats' of your tasks may be getting 'eaten' by the 'wolves' of missed deadlines and lost opportunities. So, make your meetings meaningful, or else you might find your 'goat' is gone!

M9
TALENT AND DILIGENCE
Sar Kamler

Once, a dispute arose among the gods. They argued whether Talent or Diligence would win when given equal opportunities. To settle the argument, they granted both unlimited opportunities to excel in any field of their choosing. Talent, being abundantly gifted, rose quickly to the peak of success, earning praise and admiration from all corners. Everything came naturally to him, and every task he undertook flourished into a masterpiece with an effortless ease. In contrast, Diligence progressed slowly. Each advancement was a struggle, each skill a hard-won battle. His achievements, modest in comparison to Talent's meteoric rise, were hard-earned. Yet, he persisted, his unwavering spirit concealing the trials of his journey. Having reached success quickly, Talent grew complacent. With Diligence trailing far behind, he saw no competition, no threat. Living in great comfort and luxury, he enjoyed his achievements to the fullest. Diligence, meanwhile, carried on with persistent determination. His hard work began to pay dividends, his creations gradually improved, each better than the last. Honing his skills with years of consistent work, he finally created a masterpiece that surpassed the best work Talent had ever produced. Shocked by this unexpected turn of events, Talent tried to reclaim his glory. But years of idleness had degraded his skills. His attempts were inefficient, his creations no longer held the magic they once did. Thus, the divine dispute was settled.

Modern Insight
Talent is a divine gift, but without the companion of hard work, it risks being outshined by the diligent.

M10
THE NOTHING
Unknown Author

A worn-out beggar was stretched across the road when the city's mayor happened to pass by. "Hey, you!" roared the mayor, "Why are you blocking the road by laying here? Stand up immediately! Can't you see who is passing through?" "I will only rise for someone who is superior to me," replied the beggar. "Am I not superior to you?" inquired the mayor, outraged. "By no means," said the beggar, "There are countless others above you, aren't there?" "Yes," agreed the mayor. "Correct me if I'm wrong, but you are the mayor of this city, yes?" the beggar continued. "Indeed," said the mayor. "So, should you receive a promotion, what position would you assume?" the beggar asked again. "I'd be appointed as a governor," replied the mayor. "And following that?" the beggar said. "A grand vizier." "And beyond that?" the beggar pushed again. "I would be the Prime Minister," the mayor answered, "and that's the ultimate limit. There is a king above all of us. He is the most exalted." "Let's suppose for a moment that you ascend to the role of a king. What comes next?" asked the beggar. "Nothing! There's nothing beyond that!" the mayor exclaimed, "Once a king, there's no higher position one can attain." "Well, there you have it, I am that 'nothing'."

...with nothing we depart.

Final Moral

Within this book hides a captivating riddle, the solution of which will unveil the complete concluding moral. Can you unravel it to unearth the wisdom held within?

With nothing we arrive, with nothing we depart.

_ _ _   _ _   _ _ _ _ _ _   _ _ _ _ _ _ _ _

_ _ _ _ _ _ _ _ _   _ _ ‑ _ _ _ _ _ _ _ _

_____
Proudly solved by

_____
On this date

www.ingramcontent.com/pod-product-compliance
Lightning Source LLC
Chambersburg PA
CBHW071326080526
44587CB00018B/3358